Horizons West

Anthony Mann, Budd Boetticher, Sam Peckinpah: studies
of Authorship within the Western

Jim Kitses

Indiana University Press
Bloomington and London

The Cinema One series is published by
Indiana University Press
in association with *Sight and Sound*
and the Education Department of the
British Film Institute

First United States Publication 1970

Library of Congress catalog card number: 72-97239
Standard Book Number: 253–13870–1 [cl.]
253–13871–x [pa.]

Printed in Great Britain

12 Horizons West

Contents

1: Authorship and Genre: Notes on the Western

The most popular and enduring of Hollywood forms, the western has yet received scant critical attention. Especially in recent years, it has been the director rather than the form that has occupied critical energies. Rightly so, up to a point, and much of this book springs from the desire to rescue three talented men from the neglect forced upon them. The gains resulting from the emergence of *auteur* theory have been remarkable: the beginnings of a systematic critical approach; the foundation for a subject with its own body of knowledge; the great task of re-evaluation of the American cinema under way.

But I should make clear what I mean here by *auteur* theory. In my view the term describes a basic principle and a method, no more and no less: the idea of personal authorship in the cinema and – of key importance – the concomitant responsibility to honour all of a director's works by a systematic examination in order to trace characteristic themes, structures and formal qualities. In this light the idea of the *auteur* does not seem to me to solve all our problems so much as to crystallize them. Can we speak defensibly of a director who transcends his forms? Of genre as part of the industrial complex that the film-maker must dominate? At their most simplistic *auteur* critics have insisted that there is only good work and bad, authors and others. Years ago André Bazin warned fellow critics of *Cahiers du Cinéma* about the dangers of a cult of the personality latent in a narrow approach. In my view if we are

7

to avoid this pitfall and build a body of film scholarship that is both vigorous and educationally valid, we must begin to explore the inner workings of genre. It is the belief that *auteur* theory must confront this problem that has led me to structure this book in the way that I have. In place of the reactionary notion that Hollywood directors function like the charismatic heroes of their films, I have wanted to advance the idea of an American *tradition*, of which the western seems to me an admirable and central model. However, I have not tried to catalogue the history of the genre or to chart the ebb and flow of its recent usage. In lieu of these more general approaches, I here embark on a survey of what I take to be the constituent elements of the form before going on to examine in some detail the contributions of three of its finest champions in the post-war era.

First of all, the western is American history. Needless to say, this does not mean that the films are historically accurate or that they cannot be made by Italians. More simply, the statement means that American frontier life provides the milieu and *mores* of the western, its wild bunch of cowboys, its straggling towns and mountain scenery. Of course westward expansion was to continue for over a century, the frontier throughout that period a constantly shifting belt of settlement. However, Hollywood's West has typically been, from about 1865 to 1890 or so, a brief final instant in the process. This twilight era was a momentous one: within just its span we can count a number of frontiers in the sudden rash of mining camps, the building of the railways, the Indian Wars, the cattle drives, the coming of the farmer. Together with the last days of the Civil War and the exploits of the badmen, here is the raw material of the western.

At the heart of this material, and crucial to an understanding of the gifts the form holds out to its practitioners, is an ambiguous, mercurial concept: the idea of the West. From time immemorial the West had beckoned to statesmen and poets, existing as both a direction and a place, an imperialist theme and a pastoral Utopia. Great empires developed ever westward: from Greece to Rome,

John Ford's *Rio Grande*, and a Hollywood Western set

9

from Rome to Britain, from Britain to America. It was in the West as well that the fabled lands lay, the Elysian fields, Atlantis, El Dorado. As every American schoolboy knows, it was in sailing on his passage to India, moving ever westward to realize the riches of the East, that Columbus chanced on the New World. Hand in hand with the hope of fragrant spices and marvellous tapestries went the ever-beckoning dream of life eternal: surely somewhere, there where the sun slept, was the fountain of youth.

As America began to be settled and moved into its expansionist phases, this apocalyptic and materialist vision found new expression. In his seminal study *Virgin Land*, Henry Nash Smith has traced how the West as symbol has functioned in America's history and consciousness. Is the West a Garden of natural dignity and innocence offering refuge from the decadence of civilization? Or is it a treacherous Desert stubbornly resisting the gradual sweep of agrarian progress and community values? Dominating America's intellectual life in the nineteenth century, these warring ideas were most clearly at work in attitudes surrounding figures like Daniel Boone, Kit Carson and Buffalo Bill Cody, who were variously seen as rough innocents ever in flight from society's artifice, and as enlightened pathfinders for the new nation. A folk-hero manufactured in his own time, Cody himself succumbed towards the end of his life to the play of these concepts that so gripped the imagination of his countrymen: 'I stood between savagery and civilization most all my early days.'

Refracted through and pervading the genre, this ideological tension has meant that a wide range of variation is possible in the basic elements of the form. The plains and mountains of western landscape can be an inspiring and civilizing environment, a moral universe productive of the western hero, a man with a code. But this view, popularized by Robert Warshow in his famous essay, 'The Westerner', is one-sided. Equally the terrain can be barren and savage, surroundings so demanding that men are rendered morally ambiguous, or wholly brutalized. In the same way, the community in the western can be seen as a positive force, a movement of refinement, order and local democracy into the wilds, or as a harbinger of corruption in the form of Eastern values which threaten frontier ways. This analysis over-simplifies in isolating the attitudes: a conceptually complex structure that draws on both images is the typical one. If Eastern figures such as bankers, lawyers and journalists are often either drunkards or corrupt, their female counterparts generally carry virtues and graces which the West clearly lacks. And if Nature's harmonies produce the upright hero, they also harbour the animalistic Indian. Thus central to the form we have a philosophical dialectic, an ambiguous cluster of meanings and attitudes that provide the traditional thematic structure of the genre. This shifting ideological play can be described through a series of antinomies, so:

THE WILDERNESS	CIVILIZATION
The Individual	The Community
freedom	restriction
honour	institutions
self-knowledge	illusion
integrity	compromise
self-interest	social responsibility
solipsism	democracy
Nature	Culture
purity	corruption
experience	knowledge
empiricism	legalism
pragmatism	idealism
brutalization	refinement
savagery	humanity
The West	The East
America	Europe
the frontier	America
equality	class
agrarianism	industrialism
tradition	change
the past	the future

In scanning this grid, if we compare the tops and tails of each sub-section, we can see the ambivalence at work at its outer limits:

the West, for example, rapidly moves from being the spearhead of manifest destiny to the retreat of ritual. What we are dealing with here, of course, is no less than a national world-view: underlying the whole complex is the grave problem of identity that has special meaning for Americans. The isolation of a vast unexplored continent, the slow growth of social forms, the impact of an unremitting New England Puritanism obsessed with the cosmic struggle of good and evil, of the elect and the damned, the clash of allegiances to Mother Country and New World, these factors are the crucible in which American consciousness was formed. The thrust of contradictions, everywhere apparent in American life and culture, is clearest in the great literary heritage of the romantic novel that springs from Fenimore Cooper and moves through Hawthorne and Melville, Mark Twain and Henry James, Fitzgerald and Faulkner, Hemingway and Mailer. As Richard Chase has underlined in his *The American Novel and Its Tradition*, this form in American hands has always tended to explore rather than to order, to reflect on rather than to moralize about, the irreconcilables that it confronts; and where contradictions are resolved the mode is often that of melodrama or the pastoral. For failing to find a moral tone and a style of close social observation – in short, for failing to be *English* – the American novel has often had its knuckles rapped. As with literature, so with the film: the prejudice that even now persists in many quarters of criticism and education with reference to the Hollywood cinema (paramountly in America itself) flows from a similar lack of understanding.

The ideology that I have been discussing inevitably filters through many of Hollywood's genres: the western has no monopoly here. But what gives the form a particular thrust and centrality is its historical setting; its being placed at exactly that moment when options are still open, the dream of a primitivistic individualism, the ambivalence of at once beneficent and threatening horizons, still tenable. For the film-maker who is preoccupied with these motifs, the western has offered a remarkably expressive canvas. Nowhere, of course, is the freedom that it bestows for personal expression more evident than in the cinema of John Ford.

It would be presumptuous to do more than refer here to this distinguished body of work, the crucial silent period of which remains almost wholly inaccessible. Yet Ford's career, a full-scale scrutiny of which must be a priority, stands as unassailable proof of how the historical dimensions of the form can be orchestrated to produce the most personal kind of art. As Andrew Sarris has pointed out, 'no American director has ranged so far across the landscape of the American past'. But the journey has been a long and deeply private one through green valleys of hope on to bitter sands of despair. The peak comes in the forties where Ford's works are bright monuments to his vision of the trek of the faithful to the Promised Land, the populist hope of an ideal community, a dream affectionately etched in *The Grapes of Wrath, My Darling Clementine, Wagonmaster*. But as the years slip by the darker side of Ford's romanticism comes to the foreground, and twenty years after the war – in *The Man who Shot Liberty Valance, Two Rode Together, Cheyenne Autumn* – we find a regret for the past, a bitterness at the larger role of Washington, and a desolation over the neglect of older values. The trooping of the colours has a different meaning now. As Peter Wollen has described in his chapter on *auteur* theory in *Signs and Meaning in the Cinema*, the progression can be traced in the transposition of civilized and savage elements. The Indians of *Drums Along the Mohawk* and *Stagecoach*, devilish marauders that threaten the hardy pioneers, suffer a sea-change as Ford's hopes wane, until with *Cheyenne Autumn* they are a civilized, tragic people at the mercy of a savage community. The ringing of the changes is discernible in the choice of star as well, the movement from the quiet idealism of the early Fonda through the rough pragmatism of the Wayne *persona* to the cynical self-interest of James Stewart. As Ford grows older the American dream sours, and we are left with nostalgia for the Desert.

Imperious as he is, Ford is not the western; nor is the western history. For if we stand back from the western, we are less aware of historical (or representational) elements than of form and *archetype*. This may sound platitudinous: for years critics have spoken confidently of the balletic movement of the genre, of pattern and variation, of myth. This last, ever in the air when the form is discussed, clouds the issues completely. We can speak of the genre's celebration of America, of the contrasting images of Garden and Desert, as national myth. We can speak of the parade of mythology that is mass culture, of which the western is clearly a part. We can invoke Greek and medieval myth, referring to the western hero as a latter-day knight, a contemporary Achilles. Or we can simply speak of the myth of the western, a journalistic usage which evidently implies that life is not like that. However, in strict classical terms of definition myth has to do with the activity of gods, and as such the western has no myth. Rather, it incorporates elements of *displaced* (or corrupted) myth on a scale that can render them considerably more prominent than in most art. It is not surprising that little advance is made upon the clichés, no analysis undertaken that interprets how these elements are at work within a particular film or director's career. What are the archetypal elements we sense within the genre and how do they function? As Northrop Frye has shown in his monumental *The Anatomy of Criticism,* for centuries this immensely tangled ground has remained almost wholly unexplored in literature itself. The primitive state of film criticism inevitably reveals a yawning abyss in this direction.

Certain facts are clear. Ultimately the western derives from the long and fertile tradition of Wild West literature that had dominated the mass taste of nineteenth-century America. Fenimore Cooper is again the germinal figure here: Nash Smith has traced how the roots of the formula, the adventures of an isolated, aged trapper/hunter (reminiscent of Daniel Boone) who rescues genteel heroines from the Indians, were in the *Leatherstocking Tales* which began to emerge in the 1820s. These works, fundamentally in the tradition of the sentimental novel, soon gave way to a rush of pulp literature in succeeding decades culminating in the famous series edited by Erastus Beadle which had astonishing sales for its time. Specialists in the adventure tale, the romance, the sea story, turned to the West for their setting to cash in on the huge market. As the appetite for violence and spectacle grew, variations followed, the younger hunter that had succeeded Cooper's hero losing his pristine nature and giving way to a morally ambiguous figure with a dark past, a Deadwood Dick who is finally redeemed by a woman's love. The genre, much of it sub-literary, became increasingly hungry for innovation as the century wore on, its Amazon heroines perhaps only the most spectacular sign of a desperation at its declining hold on the imagination. As the actual drama of the frontier finally came to a close, marked by Frederick C. Turner's historic address before the American Historical Association in 1893 where he advanced his thesis on free land and its continual recession westward as the key factor in America's development, the vogue for the dime novel waned, its hero now frozen in the figure of the American cowboy.

In 1900 the Wild Bunch held up and robbed a Union Pacific railway train in Wyoming; in 1903 Edwin S. Porter made *The Great Train Robbery* in New Jersey. The chronology of these events, often commented on, seems less important than their geography: it had been the East as well from which Beadle westerns such as *Seth Jones; or, The Captives of the Frontier* had flowed. The cinema was born, its novel visual apparatus at the ready, the heir to a venerable tradition of reworking history (the immediate past) in tune with ancient classical rhythms. In general, of course, the early silent cinema everywhere drew on and experimented with traditional and folkloric patterns for the forms it required. What seems remarkable about the western, however, is that the core of a formulaic lineage already existed. The heart of this legacy was romantic narrative, tales which insisted on the idealization of characters who wielded near-magical powers. Recurrent confrontations between the personified forces of good and evil, testimony to the grip of the New England Calvinist ethic, had soon focused the tales in the direction of morality play. However, in any case, the structure was an impure one which had interpolated melodramatic patterns of corruption and redemption, the revenge motif borrowed from the stage towards the end of the century, and humour in the Davy Crockett and Eastern cracker-barrel traditions. The physical action and spectacle of the Wild West shows, an offshoot of the penny-dreadful vogue, was to be another factor.

The Great Train Robbery; The Deadwood Coach

16

This complex inheritance meant that from the outset the western could be many things. In their anecdotal *The Western* George N. Fenin and William K. Everson have chronicled the proliferating, overlapping growth of early days: Bronco Billy Anderson's robust action melodramas, Thomas H. Ince's darker tales, W. S. Hart's more 'authentic' romances, the antics of the virtuous Tom Mix, the Cruze and Ford epics of the twenties, the stunts and flamboyance of Ken Maynard and Hoot Gibson, the flood of 'B' movies, revenge sagas, serials, and so on. Experiment seems always to have been varied and development dynamic, the pendulum swinging back and forth between opposing poles of emphasis on drama and history, plots and spectacle, romance and 'realism', seriousness and comedy. At any point where audience response was felt the action could freeze, the industrial machine moving into high gear to produce a cycle and, in effect, establish a minor tradition within the form. Whatever 'worked' was produced, the singing westerns of the thirties perhaps only the most prominent example of this policy of eclectic enterprise.

For many students of the western Gene Autry and Roy Rogers have seemed an embarrassing aberration. However, such a view presupposes that there is such an animal as *the* western, a precise model rather than a loose, shifting and variegated genre with many roots and branches. The word 'genre' itself, although a helpful one, is a mixed blessing: for many the term carries literary overtones of technical *rules*. Nor is 'form' any better; the western is many *forms*. Only a pluralist vision makes sense of our experience of the genre and begins to explain its amazing vigour and adaptability, the way it moves closer and further from our own world, brightening or darkening with each succeeding decade. Yet over the years critics have ever tried to freeze the genre once and for all in a definitive model of the 'classical' western. Certainly it must be admitted that works such as *Shane* and *My Darling Clementine* weld together in remarkable balance historical reconstruction and national themes with personal drama and archetypal elements. In his essay, 'The Evolution of the Western', Bazin declared *Stagecoach* the summit of the form, an example of 'classic maturity', before going on to see

Tumbleweeds with W. S. Hart; Gene Autry

in Anthony Mann's early small westerns the path of further progress. Although there is a certain logic in searching for films at the centre of the spectrum, I suspect it is a false one and can see little value in it. Wherever definitions of *the* genre movie have been advanced they have become the weapons of generalization. Insisting on the purity of his classical elements, Bazin dismisses 'superwesterns' (*Shane, High Noon, Duel in the Sun*) because of their introduction of interests 'not endemic'. Warshow's position is similar, although his conception of the form is narrower, a particular kind of moral and physical texture embodied in his famous but inadequate view of the hero as 'the last gentleman'. Elsewhere Mann's films have been faulted for their neurotic qualities, strange and powerful works such as *Rancho Notorious* have been refused entry because they are somehow 'not westerns'. This impulse may well be informed by a fear that unless the form is defined precisely (which inevitably excludes) it will disappear, wraith-like, from under our eyes. The call has echoed out over the lonely landscape of critical endeavour: what *is* the western?

The model we must hold before us is of a varied and flexible structure, a thematically fertile and ambiguous world of historical material shot through with archetypal elements which are themselves ever in flux. In defining the five basic modes of literary fiction Northrop Frye has described myth as stories about gods; romance as a world in which men are superior both to other men and to their environment; high mimetic where the hero is a leader but subject to social criticism and natural law; low mimetic where the hero is one of us; and ironic where the hero is inferior to ourselves and we look down on the absurdity of his plight. If we borrow this scale, it quickly becomes apparent that if the western was originally rooted between romance and high mimetic (characteristic forms of which are epic and tragedy), it rapidly became open to inflection in any direction. Surely the only definition we can advance of the western hero, for example, is that he is both complete and incomplete, serene and growing, vulnerable and invulnerable, a man and a god. If at juvenile levels the action approaches the near-divine, for serious artists who understand the tensions within the genre the focus can be anywhere along the scale. The directors I examine in detail later are good examples: in Anthony Mann there is a constant drive towards mythic quality in the hero; in Sam Peckinpah there is a rich creative play with the romantic potential; with Budd Boetticher it is the ironic mode that dominates.

The romantic mainstream that the western took on from pulp literature provided it with the stately ritual of displaced myth, the movement of a god-like figure into the demonic wasteland, the death and resurrection, the return to a paradisal garden. Within the form were to be found seminal archetypes common to all myth, the journey and the quest, the ceremonies of love and marriage, food and drink, the rhythms of waking and sleeping, life and death. But the incursions of melodrama and revenge had turned the form on its axis, the structure torn in the directions of both morality play and tragedy. Overlaying and interpenetrating the historical thematic there was an archetypal and metaphysical ideology as well. Manifest destiny was answered by divine providence, a Classical conception of fate brooding over the sins of man. Where history was localizing and authenticating archetype, archetype was stiffening and universalizing history.

The western thus was – and is – a complex variable, its peculiar alchemy allowing a wide range of intervention, choice and experiment by script-writer and director. History provides a source of epics, spectacle and action films, pictures sympathetic to the Indian, 'realistic' films, even anti-westerns (Delmer Daves's *Cowboy*). From the archetypal base flow revenge films, fables, tragedies, pastorals, and a juvenile stream of product. But of course the dialectic is always at work and the elements are never pure. Much that is produced, the great bulk of it inevitably undistinguished, occupies a blurred middle ground. But for the artist of vision in *rapport* with the genre, it offers a great freedom for local concentration and imaginative play.

'My name is John Ford. I make westerns.' Few film-makers can have been so serene about accepting such a label. After all, the

20

industry must have ambivalent attitudes about the 'horse-opera' which has been their bread and butter for so long. And of course the western has been at the heart of mass culture, the staple of television, its motifs decorating advertisements and politicians, the pulp fiction and comic books flowing endlessly as do the films themselves. But in fact its greatest strength has been this very pervasiveness and repetition. In this context, the western appears a huge iceberg the small tip of which has been the province of criticism, the great undifferentiated and submerged body below principally agitating the social critic, the student of mass media, the educationalist. This sharp division has been unfortunate: sociology and education have often taken up crude positions in their obliviousness to the highest achievements; criticism has failed to explore the dialectic that keeps the form vigorous. For if mass production at the base exploits the peak, the existence of that base allows refinement and reinvigoration. It is only because the western has been everywhere before us for so long that it 'works'. For over the years a highly sophisticated sub-language of the cinema has been created that is intuitively understood by the audience, a firm basis for art.

It is not just that in approaching the western a director has a structure that is saturated with conceptual significance: the core of meanings is in the imagery itself. Through usage and time, recurring elements anchored in the admixture of history and archetype and so central as to be termed *structural* – the hero, the antagonist, the community, landscape – have taken on an ever-present cluster of possible significances. To see a church in a movie – any film but a western – is to see a church; the camera records. By working carefully for it a film-maker can give that church meaning, through visual emphasis, context, repetitions, dialogue. But a church in a western has *a priori* a potential expressiveness rooted in the accretions of the past. In Ford's *My Darling Clementine* a half-built church appears in one brief scene: yet it embodies the spirit of pioneer America. Settlers dance vigorously on the rough planks in the open air, the flag fluttering above the frame of the church perched precariously on the edge of the desert.

My Darling Clementine: the half-built church

Marching ceremoniously up the incline towards them, the camera
receding with an audacious stateliness, come Tombstone's knight
and his 'lady fair', Wyatt Earp and Clementine. The community
are ordered aside by the elder as the couple move on to the floor,
their robust dance marking the marriage ceremony that unites the
best qualities of East and West. It is one of Ford's great moments.

However, the scene is not magic, but flows from an exact understanding (or intuition) of how time-honoured elements can have
the resonance of an *icon*. This term, which I borrow from art
history, should connote an image that both records and carries a
conceptual and emotional weight drawn from a *defined* symbolic
field, a tradition. Like Scripture, the western offers a world of
metaphor, a range of latent content that can be made manifest
depending on the film-maker's awareness and preoccupations.
Thus in Boetticher's *Decision at Sundown* a marriage ceremony
is completely violated by the hero who promises to kill the

The marriage ceremony: *Decision at Sundown* and *Ride the High Country*

bridegroom by nightfall. Here the meaning flows completely from the players, in particular Randolph Scott's irrational behaviour; the church itself is devoid of meaning. In Anthony Mann churches rarely appear. In Peckinpah churches have been a saloon and a brothel, and religion in characters has masked a damaging repressiveness. If we turn to the Indian we find that, apart from the early *Seminole*, he functions in Boetticher as part of a hostile universe, no more and no less. In Mann, however, the Indian is part of the natural order and as such his slaughter stains the landscape; it is not surprising that at times he comes, like an avenging spirit, to redress the balance. In Peckinpah the Indian, ushering in the theme of savagery, brings us to the very centre of the director's world.

Central to much that I have been saying is the principle of convention. I have refrained from using the term only because it is often loosely used and might have confused the issues. At times the term is used pejoratively, implying cliché; at others it is employed to invoke a set of mystical rules that the master of the form can juggle. In this light, a western is a western is a western. If we see the term more neutrally, as an area of agreement between audience and artist with reference to the form which his art will take, it might prove useful at this stage to recapitulate the argument by summarizing the interrelated aspects of the genre that I have tried to isolate, all of which are in some measure conventional.

(*a*) *History*: The basic convention of the genre is that films in western guise are about America's past. This constant tension with history and the freedom it extends to script-writer and film-maker to choose their distance is a great strength.

(*b*) *Themes*: The precise chronology of the genre and its inheritance of contradictions fundamental to the American mind dictate a rich range of themes expressed through a series of familiar character types and conflicts (e.g. law versus the gun, sheep versus cattle). These motifs, situations and characters can be the focus for a director's interests or can supply the ground from which he will quarry what concerns him.

(*c*) *Archetype*: The inherent complexity and structural confusion (or the *decadence*) of the pulp literature tradition that the western drew on from the beginning meant that westerns could incorporate elements of romance, tragedy, comedy, morality play. By a process of natural commercial selection cycles emerged and began to establish a range of forms.

(*d*) *Icons*: As a result of mass production, the accretions of time, and the dialectic of history and archetype, characters, situations and actions can have an emblematic power. Movement on the horizon, the erection of a community, the pursuit of Indians, these have a range of possible associations. Scenes such as passing on gun-lore, bathing or being barbered, playing poker, have a latent ritualistic meaning which can be brought to the surface and inflected. The quest, the journey, the confrontation, these can take on moral or allegorical overtones.

What holds all of these elements together (and in that sense provides the basis convention) is narrative and dramatic structure. It is only through mastery of these that a film-maker can both engage his audience and order the form in a personally meaningful way. At a general level this means the understanding and control necessary for any expression of emotion in terms of film – the creating of fear, suspense, amusement, awe. However, with an art as popular as the western this must also mean a precise awareness of audience expectation with reference to a range of characters – pre-eminently hero and antagonist – and testing situations, conflicts, spectacle, landscape, physical action and violence. Fundamental to success would seem to be the understanding that the world created must be essentially fabulous. While treating situations that have their relevance for us, the form must not impinge too directly on our experience. The world that the film creates is self-contained and its own; it comments not on our life but on the actions and relationships it reveals to us. So long as the world evoked is *other*, few limitations exist. A commonplace about the form, that it is handy for exploring simple moral issues, does not survive the experience of attending to any number of works: the maturity of relationships in Robert Parrish's *Wonderful Country*, the complex moral and metaphysical rhetoric of *Johnny Guitar*, the work, certainly, of the three directors studied in this book, these could hardly be called simple. Nor are social and psychological elements impossible so long as they are held in a fruitful tension with the romantic thrust of the genre. *Showdown at Boot Hill*, where Charles Bronson has become a bounty hunter because he

The Left-handed Gun

feels he is too *short*, is an unsuccessful Freudian tale. *The Left-handed Gun*, where the murder of a father-figure turns Billy the Kid anti-social and self-destructive, is a distinguished psychological tragedy. *3.10 to Yuma* and *Shane*, both maligned because of their success where the genre proper fails (i.e. with most film journalists), are honourable works. Rather than dogma, the grounds must be quality. And the challenge always is to find the dramatic structure that best serves both film-maker and audience.

The western is not just the men who have worked within it. Rather than an empty vessel breathed into by the film-maker, the genre is a vital structure through which flow a myriad of themes and concepts. As such the form can provide a director with a range of possible connections and the space in which to experiment, to shape and refine the kind of effects and meanings he is working towards. We must be prepared to entertain the idea that *auteurs* grow, and that genre can help to crystallize preoccupations and contribute actively to development. Moreover, we must be clear about directors who return to the western time and again. To work with 'stark reality' (Boetticher's phrase) may be the dream of many a Hollywood film-maker; yet it does not follow that the closer he comes to articulating private worlds directly, the higher the achievement. Certainly the western compels distance if the result is to be both personal and commercially viable. Bazin came to praise both Mann and Boetticher for returning to what he felt was the essence of the genre in their small revenge movies. But in my view the reverse is true: these two men, together with Sam Peckinpah, can be said to have found *their* essence within the western.

2: Anthony Mann: the Overreacher

If Christ hadn't risen there would have been no story. – Anthony Mann

From The Great Flamarion to the Cid, from beginning to end, the characters of Anthony Mann are extreme men stretching out beyond their reach. Rarely is it a matter of choice; as if possessed, these men push ahead completely at the mercy of forces within themselves. Whether apocalyptic or divine, the vessels of a vision or a disturbance, they have little hope of the settled relationships within which most men live. Typically, they are driven to sacrifice or reject the complex ties of family and society; often, they are *usurpers*.

Given this perspective, it is clear that the significance of Mann's first commercial and artistic success, *T-Men*, has been misunderstood. Location work was always to be important to Mann (*T-Men* was his first project shot outside the studio, by no means commonplace in 1947), and here he seized on the freedom to script and film a subject as he liked. For ten years Mann had been waiting in the wings, an apprentice to the cheap second-feature. But although its urban atmosphere is notable, *T-Men*'s force flows directly from a structure which requires its young heroes to penetrate a sinister counterfeiting gang. As the married agent, Alfred Ryder consequently finds himself forced to play the role to the hilt, first denying his wife when she comes upon him in a market in his undercover *persona*, and then his partner, Dennis O'Keefe, who has to support the gang, his own disguise intact, as they destroy his fellow agent.

29

This kind of tragic paradox was always to fascinate Mann. In all his thrillers of the late forties Mann evoked two worlds diametrically opposed, one of innocence and purity, the other an evil domain which extracts a sacrifice in its defeat. Nowhere was this interaction more harshly in evidence than in *Border Incident*, Mann capitalizing on the success of *T-Men* by adapting its structure to the subject of an immigration racket operating in the American South-West. However, here the melodrama was radically extended by an elemental violence, one agent ground into a field by a tractor, the other nearly suffocating nightmarishly in quicksand. If the city never offered Mann the setting to extend his talents, the terrain of *Border Incident*, shaping the narrative and bringing alive the action, clearly did. In a fragmented way (like *T-Men*, the film has a documentary framework), the metaphorical drive of the imagery – especially in its climax where gangsters march along the rim of a steep canyon through which wind peasants on their way to the slaughter – gives *Border Incident* an almost symbolic level of action. Promising a thriller, Mann delivers something of a cosmic conflict which hints at the play of superhuman forces that can shape destiny.

It was in the western that Mann was to weld together themes, structure and style to produce his most personal works. The drive towards enlarged character and heightened conflict found its natural canvas in the genre. His first efforts, the downbeat Indian picture, *Devil's Doorway*, and *The Furies*, a reworking of Dostoevsky's *The Idiot* which I have not been able to see, were dispiriting box-office failures. But *Winchester '73* was a major break-through, sparking off the partnerships with Borden Chase and James Stewart, securing Mann's place within the industry, and announcing definitively his artistic arrival. In the fifties Mann was to be at his most prolific and creative; eighteen movies in all, eleven of them westerns, the great majority both bearing his personal stamp and enjoying some commercial success. Throughout the period Mann was to advance steadily, growing in authority as his distinctive vision found expression, progressively extending his reach over the years to embrace colour, CinemaScope, more ambitious productions, until finally he stood on the threshold of the epic.

Dominating the earlier half of the decade was Mann's remarkable collaboration with James Stewart through eight films. The quality that anchored Mann's respect for Stewart was the actor's dedication, his preparing for *Winchester '73*, for example, by spending hours firing the gun; later Mann was to speak admiringly of Stewart's readiness to do virtually anything from staging a fight under horses' hooves to allowing himself to be dragged through a fire. This single-mindedness, interlocking with Mann's conception of character, provided the natural vehicle for the director's themes. Animating the obsessive heroes of the westerns, the idealistic characters of *Thunder Bay*, *The Glenn Miller Story*, *Strategic Air Command*, Stewart revealed an emotional range unlooked-for given his early career of light comedy roles. However, the charming, bemused side of the actor's talent was also important to Mann, in the westerns humour expressing the cynicism and softening the violent edge of the character, in the other films the amusing vagueness and corn-ball jokes disguising the ruthlessness of a hero callously subordinating the rights of others to his private goal.

Mann's work outside the western was often uneven, evidence of an unsureness in reconciling thematic drives with material: it is difficult to deify a trombone-player, no matter how good he was. Similarly, *Serenade*, a bizarre operatic study of the threats that modern society holds for natural passion, took Mann to the upper reaches of melodrama with Mario Lanza living out the tragedy of his stage role as Otello. Only with *God's Little Acre* (I have not seen *Men in War*, which has its reputation) did Mann in this period approach the vigour and coherence of his best work within the western, the setting of the Old South, the Biblical undertones of the material, the violent conflicts of a divided family close to the soil, combining to provide the director with the structure and action he required.

If the genre was never to be quite the same for his work within it, in films like *The Naked Spur*, *The Last Frontier*, and *Man of the West* Mann arrived at the summit of his personal authority and expressiveness. The dynamic interplay of the concepts of individualism and communal responsibility within the form allowed

The Glenn Miller Story and *Winchester '73:* two contrasting sides of James Stewart

32

Mann to return time and again to the strange neo-classic conflict of passion and duty that was always to preoccupy him. Mann was never to resolve the tension; and his fascination for the charismatic individual, the superior man, led him finally to the idea of transcendence, and, inevitably, the epic. Crucial, therefore, was the ambiguity of the western's own attitudes towards these concepts, providing a structure of fruitful tension within which it was possible to achieve an art both personal and integrated. Equally important were the settings of the West which were to allow the gradual refinement of Mann's distinctively physical style, and an unparalleled opportunity to explore through the dialectic of landscape and hero the interior and finally *metaphysical* conflict of his characters.

The Hero

Well actually he was a man who could kill his own brother. . . .

Characteristically, the Mann hero is a revenge hero. This is the basic drive Mann imbues his characters with, regardless of the narrative pattern. At the formal level, revenge is at the centre of only two works, *Winchester '73* and *The Man from Laramie*, although it affects the denouement of three others as well, *Bend of the River*, *The Far Country* and *Man of the West*. If we set aside *Devil's Doorway*, *The Last Frontier* and *Cimarron* – three films that I propose to consider separately here – this leaves (apart from *The Furies*) *The Naked Spur* and *The Tin Star*, in both of which the protagonist flees a past of emotional hurt by becoming a bounty hunter. This pattern of denial is a key one, since it is a pure expression of the characteristic drive of the Mann hero. For the revenge taken by the character is taken upon *himself*, a punishment the inner meaning of which is a denial of reason and humanity. In general, all of Mann's heroes behave as if driven by a vengeance they must inflict upon themselves for having once been human, trusting and, therefore, vulnerable. Hence the schizophrenic style of the hero, the violent explosions of passion alternating with precarious moments of quiet reflection.

Typically the hero has a highly developed moral sense while

being at the mercy of an irrational drive to deny that very side of his nature. The hero also has a strong sense of chivalry, society's cloak for instinct and strong feeling, which vanishes when he is under stress. These tensions, extended in the structure of the films, make of the Mann hero a microcosm of the community, where ideals, reason and humanity are always prominent but below which lie self-interest, passion and violence. Passion, the special quality of the hero, suggests the directions in which he is driven – an assertion of the self above all other things, a movement towards the solitary status of a demi-god, the private and invulnerable world of madness, the total freedom of death. Dark, extreme men trapped in an impossible dilemma, a neurotic attempt to escape themselves and rise above a past of pain and violence, Mann's heroes are *brought low*, driven by forces over which they have no control to face themselves, reliving the very experiences they flee.

Like the plaything of a cruel world, the Mann hero is ever at the mercy of paradox and contradiction. Lin McAdam of *Winchester '73* is a model of stability and decorum in all respects except where his own brother is concerned, the mere sight of whom dements the character. *Bend of the River* centres on the attempts of Glyn McLyntock to reject his past as a badman, the character slowly forced into a situation where, his rational exterior shattered, he must destroy a man who shares that past and is virtually a blood brother. Mann was to return to this structure (six years later, in 1958) with *Man of the West*, where the hero is driven to kill both stepbrother and stepfather before he can lay the ghost of his origins and preserve his hard-won status of peaceful citizen. Gary Cooper's Link Jones rarely has the hysteria that Stewart brought to the role, the peak of which was in *The Naked Spur* where in his efforts to turn bounty hunter Howie Kemp borders on the unbalanced. Similarly, Henry Fonda's Morg Hickman of *The Tin Star* is a softer character, although his situation is identical with Kemp's. Driven in an unnatural direction, away from the community, the hero is morally ambiguous, his actions carrying a nihilistic undertone. *The Far Country* makes the crisis explicit, Jeff Webster

35

The Man from Laramie: James Stewart as Will Lockhart

irrationally insisting on his isolation ('I don't need other people') despite the evidence of his commitment to Ben, his older side-kick.

Mann's heroes find themselves outside the community because of deeply personal wounds. McAdam pursues the killer of his father, his own brother, while Link Jones has been torn from society because of his past with the gang of Dock Tobin, his evil stepfather. Fonda's Morg Hickman has been embittered by the community's indifference which resulted in the death of his wife and child, Kemp has turned to bounty hunting to find the money to buy back the ranch his faithless fiancée sold out from under him, and, more generally, Webster trusted a woman 'once'. The persistence of this kind of motivation, disturbance within the family unit in a distant past, is one source of the compulsive charge the hero carries, and gives the action a predetermined quality. In *The Man from Laramie*, most notably, the feeling created is of an ancestry that inevitably shapes what will come to pass. The Stewart character here, Will Lockhart, has left his army post to find whoever sold the rifles to the Apache who killed his brother. His persistence slowly begins to crack open the sources of evil in the Waggoman family and old Alec, taking on Lockhart's mission, brings himself face to face with the facts: that Vic, his foster-son, is prepared to murder him, that Vic and Dave, his natural son, sold the rifles, that he himself has brought it all about through his ambition and power.

This psychological action is central to Mann's films and the source of their symmetry and moral complexity. Thus when Lockhart finally confronts his enemy over the rifles he cannot kill Vic, who is basically a rational, amiable man with some justification for his acts – in short, a man very much like Lockhart. This tension is at the centre of *Bend of the River* where McLyntock, despite his suspicions, hopes that the Arthur Kennedy character wants to join him in leaving a criminal life behind. But Cole, created in the film almost as an *alter ego* to McLyntock, slips the other way and forces division. Ironically, the former Missouri raider is driven to take up the stance of his past, preying on the wagon train that Cole has usurped and drowning his friend in a murderous struggle

38

before he is free. Similarly, both Morg Hickman and Howie Kemp re-create their past even as they try to bury it. Hickman, an ex-marshal, takes lodgings with a widow and her child and is slowly drawn into the lawman problems of the young Owens. Kemp finds himself involved with Lina, a morally doubtful character whom he comes to care for despite anxieties which are naturally bolstered when she betrays him, forced to it to save his life.

Mann's heroes are always empirical men, distrustful of idealism or generalization. Facile appeals to principle or feelings are met laconically: 'Oh, yeah?' Simple explanations of suspect happenings – the murder of innocents disguised as self-defence, double-dealing masquerading as the law – generate a similar circumspection. Knowledge is a pragmatic thing, born of experience. Judgements based on appearances are worthless, and meaningful action with all its heavy costs is not entered into lightly. In fact Mann's characters are reluctant heroes, rarely *deciding* to act. With Morg Hickman of *The Tin Star* Mann was able to emphasize the empirical side of his hero, Henry Fonda perfectly embodying the knowledge and skills that only experience can bestow. Oddly domestic for a Mann hero, Hickman is in some measure the most mature version of the type as well. Far removed from the hysteria of a Howie Kemp, Hickman's basic quality is one of resignation, a sad awareness of what the world is like. It is only the character's occasional bitter-ness that makes credible his occupation, the role of bounty hunter sitting uneasily on one so warmly committed to human worth. Like *The Man from Laramie*, *The Tin Star* is built round a transfer of role and qualities from the hero to a secondary character who only gradually emerges as the focus for our experience of the action. With Alec Waggoman and Lockhart it is a case of age, arrogance and power being checked by moral doubt and a drive for the truth inspired by the younger man. But with *The Tin Star*, the pattern is more complex, the idealism of youth being stiffened by the wisdom and power that is passed on by Hickman, who in turn is forced to face himself through the example of Owens. In both cases the younger man fills out the psychological structure, functioning both as something of a son to the older and as an

Psychological structure: *Bend of the River* and *The Tin Star*

← *Man of the West:* Link Jones (Gary Cooper) and Coaley (Jack Lord)

embodiment of his youth, and in this way triggering action and change.

Mann often deceives by introducing his men as simple, uncluttered heroes, the mood slowly darkening as we notice similarities in temperament and behaviour between hero and villain. Hence Link Jones of *Man of the West* who appears a country bumpkin at the outset, only to emerge later as capable of the most brutal of acts, savagely beating and tearing the pants off the wolfish young Coaley. The extraordinary power of this famous scene, which culminates in Link not being quite able to strangle his beaten and humiliated opponent with his bare hands, flows again from what I have called the psychological structure in Mann's work. For in attempting to destroy the past that holds him to ransom – tangibly, in that Coaley is created in the film as Link's successor – the hero is driven inescapably to relive it, the violence and evil that he has tried to bury forced to surface by the situation he is in. Here Mann underlines the moral ambiguity of his hero, giving weight and integrity to John Dehner's Claude, the stepbrother who will not hear of running out on the crazed Dock: 'I watch out for that old man. I love him, and I watch out for him.'

A similar complexity was achieved by Mann in the first Stewart western, *Winchester '73*, where the affable McAdam finally gives way to the hysterical hero of the end. The structure here is less elaborate (perhaps because of the limitations of the original material) but effective, the opening contest for the weapon vividly evoking the competition between the brothers as well as identifying the Winchester with their father. Consequently, the brief scene of contorted violence that follows where Dutch steals the gun has considerable force, since Lin is compelled to experience a symbolic re-enactment of his brother's crime and to live through a parody of their childhood relationship, the bigger boy bullying the smaller out of his possessions. The structure is finally resolved in McAdam being driven to re-create the evil of his brother's act – the killing of kin – before he can rest.

If Howie Kemp of *The Naked Spur* and Jeff Webster of *The Far Country* are the most explicit versions of the Mann hero, Jones and

McAdam are the most developed in that both are successful in their terms. And finally we must ask what kind of success it is that accounts for the destruction of a father or brother, and how this equips the character for a role within the community. On this score the films are mute. The question may appear an external moral consideration: yet it is thrown up by the films themselves and is central to an understanding of the Mann hero. In the films I have been discussing the central character moves through conflict until at the end he is ostensibly a part of the community. But the paradox here is that his movement is resolutely *away* from the community, and we rarely witness a process we could call *growth* in the character. If there is a strong didactic tone often present – articulated in *The Tin Star*, but more characteristically felt in *The Naked Spur* and *The Far Country* – it is the result of the hero being literally *beaten* into line; we feel that 'he's learned his lesson'. His old partner shot in the back and he himself nearly shot to pieces, Jeff Webster 'chooses' a revenge that also saves the community. Exhausted from the unnatural struggle to tear his dead bounty from the torrent, crying as he slumps against his horse, loving and loved despite himself, Howie Kemp gives in: 'Do you still want to go to California?' Entry into the community can thus feel like *defeat*, the hero not so much integrated as exhausted by his compulsion to pursue an unnatural course, not educated so much as beaten by a struggle against profound forces that operate as a kind of immutable law. It is this lack of development on a moral scale, together with the insistence on psychological structure, that gives Mann's world its closed, frozen quality, his heroes their neurotic flavour. If choice is really not possible, then success becomes ambiguous. McAdam exhausted in the streets of Abilene after killing his brother, Jones driving quietly away from his family's corpses, Glyn McLyntock emerging from a rushing stream that carries his friend's body – these men seem nothing more than empty shells.

Three neglected works, *Devil's Doorway*, *The Last Frontier* and *Cimarron*, are relevant here. Spanning the period under discussion, these differ from the films thus far considered in that they focus on inversions of the typical hero. Essentially, the central characters here are stable, controlled, healthy men; and as such – paradoxically – there is no place for them within the community. Thus in the sadly overlooked and surprisingly tough Indian picture, *Devil's Doorway*, Robert Taylor's Broken Lance, the Shoshone chief who as a Union soldier had won a Congressional Medal of Honour, now finds that under the Homesteading Act Indians cannot own land. 'Civilization's a great thing.' Attempts to petition the government fail, and Lance is driven to lead his few braves in a pathetic defence of their home against a local posse bolstered by Union Cavalry. His dream of a model community shattered, the idealistic Lance dons his old uniform and moves out into the wreckage to take a bullet and walk, more dead than alive, to the officer opposite who salutes him before he dies. Here Mann had a character of great purity and elemental drive. Society cannot contain such a man, and accordingly the hero is deified, becoming a kind of mythic spirit. As in *El Cid* ten years later, the film ends on a strange note of dark exaltation – victory through death – and celebrates the uncompromising quality of the character.

This situation is reversed in the very attractive *The Last Frontier*, virtually an imaginative remake of *Devil's Doorway*, where the centre of the action is trapper Jed Cooper. Brilliantly created by Victor Mature as a bearish savage, a 'natural man', Jed becomes intrigued with the idea of wearing a Cavalry uniform despite the warnings of Gus that 'calamitous times' are upon them with the approach of civilization. Cooper is opposed by Robert Preston's Colonel Marston, the natural morality of the trapper soon coming into conflict with the martinet's 'civilized' and neurotic drive towards success. The hero begins by defeating the community, his conquest of the Colonel's lady no less than an assault on its very citadel, a fact made clear by the cutting which juxtaposes the scene with a coup by one of Red Cloud's braves, a single-handed attack on the fort. But Jed's act of leaving the Colonel to die in a bear-trap when he will not renounce his plans to destroy the Apache at all costs is frowned on by the settlement, including Anne Bancroft's Mrs Marston: 'Not *that* way.' Unmanned by civilization but now

The Last Frontier: Jed (Victor Mature) with Gus and Mungo

caught fast in its 'snares', Cooper is forced to accept the values, seen as self-destructive, of the community. The tone of the film, which has some remarkably funny moments, progressively darkens, Cooper first losing the elemental side of his nature in Mungo, his Indian side-kick who returns to the mountains, and then Gus, the wise voice of reason, who dies at the head of Marston's cavalry charge. The ending (which seems to have been imposed on Mann) is jarringly optimistic, the Colonel's wife looking on happily as Cooper in uniform salutes the flag. But the statement of the film remains clear: crossing the frontier means leaving whisky and bearskins, passion and rational simplicity behind.

It is less easy to draw any conclusions about *Cimarron*, Mann's last western in 1960, which he felt deeply bitter about since after half the picture had been shot on location the production was pulled back into M.G.M. studios and the script altered. Most notably, Yancey Cravat's death heroically fighting an oil fire was cut, the

45

hero dying off-stage in the First World War in the released version. The mutilations are unfortunate since, as with Peckinpah's *Major Dundee*, the film seems a strikingly personal epic on the origins of America. As the embodiment of the crusader and pioneer spirit of the nation, Glenn Ford tries to balance the roles of restless adventurer and idealistic newspaperman married to a demanding Maria Schell. Shooting off to fight in Cuba for five years, Yancey returns only to vanish again when his wife argues that he should compromise his ideals and accept a shady bargain which would cheat the Indians (whom he has always championed) of their oil rights in order to become Governor of the State. The irreconcilable sides of Yancey's personality are represented within the structure of the film by Pegler, the crusading father-figure from whom Yancey inherits the newspaper, and The Cherokee Kid, a young side-kick who has always idolized him but refuses to leave the disreputable life they once shared. A similar opposition exists between Anne Baxter's tough Dixie, an old friend of Yancey's from his whoring days, and his wife Sabra, who is compelled to lay aside her starry-eyed preoccupations with gentility when faced with a crisis, Mercedes McCambridge getting her hilariously drunk as she gives birth to Yancey's son. Despite the implications of The Cherokee Kid's death and his resistance to Dixie's charms, Yancey is never tamed, and the film celebrates the free expression of his pioneering impulses. The last shot is of a bronzed statue of the hero, his spirit enshrined for ever as a symbol of early America. How much was improvised by M.G.M. executives anxious to bring the sprawling picture to a halt remains an open question. But Mann's original design is clear and supports the general pattern: the values carried by his heroes, and the forces that drive them, do not find an easy home within the community.

The Villain

All Mann's characters exist on a moral and psychological grid, the main determinants of which are goodness and evil, reason and un-reason, power and weakness. This is one source of the resemblance between hero and villain, at the very least a sharing of certain characteristics, often a blood relationship. In general, hero and villain are extreme men, the villain a more or less unbalanced version of the hero, and the action of the film is a cancelling out, a neutralizing movement towards moderation, compromise and control. This is evidently an ideal state, reason and humanity being seen as attributes of natural order. However, a key source of tension and complexity is that although moral virtue carries the traditional weight of a positive value, it is never seen to bestow power which remains the property of ambiguous and extreme men.

This structure of resonance between hero and villain is central to Mann's best work. Its lack of force in *Devil's Doorway* and *Cimarron*, both relatively social films that centre on racial prejudice, results in a diminished drama. *The Tin Star* is more successful in this context, although the film is not a major one, nowhere displaying the sense of passionate engagement that is characteristic of Mann. The director suffered some interference on the production; this must have been a bitter pill to swallow given that making the film had caused a rupture between Mann and both Borden Chase and Stewart who wanted him for *Night Passage*. However, the film does have its qualities and not the least of these is the conflict between Owens and Bart Bogardus. Portrayed with appropriately unhinged malice by Neville Brand, the latter rises above the stock figure of racist to emerge as a representative of the soft under-belly of society, the hysteria and violence that both the town elders and the youthful sheriff deny in their preoccupation with ideals of decency and fair-play. This gives the climax of *The Tin Star* a fine sharpness, Anthony Perkins bringing a properly hysterical edge to his bullying of the bully. The full effect of the scene, however, depends on our awareness that the hysteria is not wholly feigned, that Owens is confronting *himself*. The moment is deeply satisfying since we have been involved with Owens's education; but our pleasure at the success of Hickman's teaching ('Study men – a gun's only a tool') should not obscure the fact that the youth has broken through to a realm of ambiguous power – he has become a killer. The roots of villainy in Mann's films always underline that although society may deny it, the exercise of such power is necessary. But in his best work Mann goes further, suggesting that the use of that power is *tragic*.

There is a fruitful tension between these two related ideas that run throughout much of Mann. On the one hand there is the view that power is neutral. Mann is clearly fascinated by the way in which knowledge and experience, independence and judgement, organization and physical prowess, can be used equally for good or ill. A particularly fine example is Roy Anderson's brilliant use of military tactics in *The Naked Spur* to bring about the liquidation of the Blackfeet so that he can continue with Kemp's party and share in the reward. But the theme is most prominent in the Chase-scripted films, explicit in the first two works and clearly there in *The Far Country* with Mr Gannon, as everyone calls him, whose organizational skill and administration are remarkable. Using the law to his advantage in Skagway, Gannon sells supplies to miners headed for the gold strike in Dawson – one of his statutes usefully insisting each miner must carry one hundred pounds of the expensive goods – and then robs and kills them on their return (the pattern recalls *Border Incident*). Both Anderson and Gannon are highly intelligent and rational villains whose presence highlights the 'limitations' (the ethical awareness) of their opposite numbers. As Gannon says with heavy sarcasm of Jeff when the showdown comes: 'We always knew he'd turn into a public-minded citizen.' Some Mann villains – most of the Dock Tobin gang (barring Claude), Ben in *The Naked Spur*, Waco of *Winchester '73* – are so far out, so unbalanced, that they seem unaware of rules of conduct. The insanity we sense in characters like Roy and Gannon, however, derives from the rational and efficient way they break rules they are aware of and disdain. The attractiveness of these characters is that they are so purely out of joint. These more refined versions of the Mann villain – naked power without a moral dimension, self-interest breeding totalitarianism – are persuasive arguments for the existence of evil. Faced with them a society cannot but sanction force, killing if necessary, the doer freed from blame by virtue of his instrumental role as vehicle for social justice.

Yet alongside this view there exists an older idea which, although it has lost ground, continues to influence our culture, and is persistently at work in Mann's films. I refer to the metaphysical concept, rooted in religion, myth and folklore, that the taking of a life is a *sacred* act. Essentially brothers under the skin, we kill at our peril, destroying a part of ourselves, staining our hands with the blood of the victim for ever thereafter. *Thou shalt not kill.* The imperative is an absolute one: there are no mitigating circumstances. Within the western this ancient precept is present in a corrupted form, the constraints surrounding the killing of a defenceless or weaker man, one of the most tenacious of conventions in the genre. Mann returns to this ritualistic situation often, in both *The Naked Spur* and *The Man from Laramie,* the enflamed hero quivering with hand on gun, but finally turning away in disgust; Link Jones's inability to strangle Coaley is another example. If we are to kill, we require situations in which we do not have to face ourselves, the decision taken out of our hands. In *The Last Frontier* this issue is at the centre of the action, Mann underlining the fact that even when disaster threatens, social sanctions are not enough to justify execution. The extremity of the act forces a communal guilt unless it has a properly ceremonial or chivalric dress. The horns of the dilemma become intolerably, unspeakably clear with the theme of parricide. What is one to do with an *evil father?* The archetypal and tragic aspects of the crisis are revealed: every man his own Hamlet.

This thematic complex seems to have provided a nexus for Borden Chase and Mann, and accounts for their creative collaboration over *Winchester '73, Bend of the River* and *The Far Country.* As a script-writer Chase seems an *auteur* in his own right, his work with other directors marked by the strong thematic interests – the archetypal conflict, the uses of power – he shared with Mann. Thus *Backlash,* directed with little force by John Sturges, none the less has an enviable punch given its narrative built round a hero determined to revenge his father who was apparently massacred when a partner failed to return with help. Obsessively pursuing his prey, Richard Widmark moves through various adventures to discover the renegade about to ambush and

wipe out a whole community; it is, of course, his father. *Red River* (which Chase co-scripted) is also relevant, the action there turning on the rebellion of Montgomery Clift against the older John Wayne figure who has taught him all that he knows. Once again the conflict is set against a broader canvas, the historic cattle drive, and the continuity of the community is seen as dependent upon the resolution of the struggle between the two men. It is this symmetry of structure, Chase's insistence on a *social* extension of the personal drama, that provides the marker to the boundaries between writer and director, and assists us in reaching a fuller understanding of Mann's work.

A basic convention of the genre, always in the foreground with Chase, sets hero and villain off through the power that they share. Thus in *Backlash*, a film that recalls *Winchester '73* at every turn, father and son both measure the effectiveness of a gun by the way it rests in the hand. For Chase prowess suggests a moral ambiguity, and is generally emblematic of an internal disturbance that poises a character on the margins of the community. In turning the skills they hold in common against the villain – who imperils the social structure – the hero thus at once achieves an inner peace, preserves the community, and establishes himself within it. A recurrent structure within the western, apparently constricting and formulaic, this pattern provides a good example of the latitude the genre allows the veteran Hollywood director. Thus for Hawks in *Red River* the relationships between the characters dominate the action, the community theme remaining abstract. Although the cattle drive is referred to as gruelling and is equated with the salvation of the territory, the epic potential of the drive is not realized in the images. The archetypal aspects of the structure are similarly undercut, the patriarchal figure of Walter Brennan functioning primarily as an onlooker and comic relief, the John Ireland character emerging as another professional rather than a kind of brother to Clift, the tragic potential of the Wayne/Clift relationship transmuted into the Hawksian drama of separation from the group. Violence becomes a form of communication – women slapping men, men beating each other to express their love – and the prowess carried

Devil's Doorway: 'If we are to kill we require situations in which we do not have to face ourselves'

by major characters a badge of their professionalism rather than a sign of interior disturbance.

In contrast with Hawks, Mann was to fasten precisely on those areas within Chase's material that allowed for an archetypal extension of the drama. Ironically, in one sense the effect was the same, the socially conscious Chase's interests in the community again fading. Thus in *Bend of the River* the theme of the need for a rationale for force is not fully developed, young Trey failing to cohere as a character, the motif clouded by Mann's handling of the end. The hysteria with which Glyn replies to Cole's treachery is something more than an expression of the precariousness of the character's ties with the community: Cole's betrayal is like self-betrayal, the betrayal of a brother, unnatural, wounding, and leading irrevocably to the murderous combat of the river. *Winchester '73*, much the best of the Mann/Chase westerns, benefits immensely through the splitting of the villainy between Waco, strikingly created by Dan Duryea, and Dutch Henry Brown. From the beginning Mann creates an opposition between Lin and Dutch, the brothers holding in common the same skill and shooting style with irreconcilable views of life. But Lin is also set off against Waco Johnnie, the conflict here resulting from the two men carrying a similar psychopathic edge, Lin's functioning in relation to Dutch and Waco – who, as Lola says, isn't 'people' – while Waco's stylish terror operates in reverse, on members of the community. Lin's destruction of Waco is consequently a key moment since it both satisfies our moral expectations and *disturbs* them, our identification with the hero jarred by the naked violence with which he sets about the villain. This is appropriate since the death of Waco is only a step towards the more personal duel with Dutch, a structure which, if less pleasing on the formal level, remains true to the drive of the character and gives the film a considerable intensity. Here again the result is that the social theme concerning the applications of power ('He didn't teach you to shoot people in the back') is obscured, the moral justification for the destruction of Dutch, his own marauding, his ruling of Waco who menaces the social structure, less prominent than the fact that Lin has no choice – he *must* kill his brother. Mann underlines this, as in *Bend of the River*, by making the final confrontation an elemental struggle, the blood pounding in the hero's head as he pits himself against his double high in the rocks. This, together with Mann's emphasis on the villain as a source of unnatural acts, lifts the action free of social or moral contexts. A dark vessel through which blow winds of an immutable justice, the hero restores order, paradoxically and tragically, by descending into the world of the villain.

In comparison with *Winchester '73*, *The Far Country* is formally perfect, yet a minor work. The film is built round a careful set of oppositions: corrupt Skagway and the emerging community of Dawson; the motifs of gold, which 'drives a man crazy', and food, especially coffee, which comes to represent neighbourliness and sharing; Ronda who balances Jeff in looking after herself, and Renée who believes that helping other people is part of living. But the key opposition is between the fascistic Gannon, who represents the logical outcome of that half of Jeff that rejects the community, and the paternal Ben, Jeff's partner, who evokes human and democratic ideals. This familar structure ensures that the resolution of the action – Jeff's solipsism leading to Ben's death which then drives him to destroy Gannon – has Mann's characteristic intensity. But the source of that intensity remains below the surface, the action of the film finally blurred by the social and moral issues that the script insists on.

However, *The Naked Spur* and *Man of the West*, Mann's most sustained works, are films of extraordinary power, their roots the wholly private quality of the heroes' struggle. Here the relationship between hero and villain is either arbitrary and therefore compulsively necessary – Howie Kemp's pursuit of Ben Vandergroat – or a family affair, as with Link and his stepfather, and thus again dictated. There is no question of larger motives. In fact the mute intensity engendered by *The Naked Spur* springs precisely from the paradox that although Kemp may be doing something socially useful, he is transgressing natural law: he is *unclean*. In both films the threat of villain to community is not at the centre of the action, the social order only suggested by the figures of the

brutalized women, Lina and Billie, and the petty thieves, Jesse and Beasley.

The latter are evidently examples of the harmless scoundrel – carpet-bagger, morally unstable prospector – that the society can accommodate. Basically good and likeable men, the characters' flaw is that they are weak. These men, like the community itself, are far removed from the world of hero and villain, the world of power. And for Mann power is something more than Chase's expertise, or the capacity for good and evil it bestows. This is involved, as are the key drives of ambition and pride: 'I knew Madden couldn't take him,' says Gannon with some satisfaction as he prepares to face Jeff. But finally the essential otherness that hero and villain share is a mysterious extremity of nature, a singularity and integrity of spirit.

Mann consistently heightens and exploits aspects of ritual and legend behind basic conventions of the genre – skill in battle, knowledge of the savage, fearlessness in the face of the unknown – to give his major characters an almost *magical* quality and a mythical stature. Hence the competition for the perfect weapon, the brothers matching each other shot for shot until the hero wins with the perfect shot, blowing a hole through a postage stamp pasted over a ring thrown in the air. 'It worked, didn't it?' asks Roy Anderson, emerging from cover after the last Indian is dead. The massacre is so total that finally it seems less a demonstration of efficient tactics than a display of diabolical power, a kind of black magic. Even in *The Tin Star*, where the drift of the script is to demystify the figure of the gunfighter, shifting attention from mechanical skill to human qualities, Mann nevertheless gives Fonda a mysterious aura, making of him the solitary keeper of the keys. In this light Owens's education becomes an introduction to secret rites, an initiation, a passing on, again, of magic. The same idea is there in *Bend of the River* where Laura admires the song of night birds, and McLyntock and Cole sardonically agree as they listen to the Indians approaching the camp; moments later the men melt into the landscape to defeat the Indians with their own methods. Men at this level instantly recognize each other:

55

Man of the West: Dock Tobin (Lee J. Cobb) and Billie Ellis (Julie London)

'I'm gonna like you,' opines Gannon after a remark or two from Webster. Gannon having stolen Jeff's cattle, Jeff steals them back, and the two men jockey expertly in the dark, aware of each other's every move, as lesser men die. 'You act as if you belong with those people,' exclaims the incredulous Sam Beasley as Link savagely digs a grave outside Dock Tobin's squalid shack. Ordinary men soon sense the differences.

Hero and villain. The kind of possibilities these structural elements presented Mann is most clear in *Man of the West.* Like Peckinpah's *Ride the High Country,* the film is built round the tragic implications of the growth of civilization; like that work, it is a personal achievement of the highest order. The film is remarkable for the integrity it allows its characters: not only Julie London's Billie, whose own precarious defences must be stripped away; or Beasley, whose cowardice is irrationally overcome when he steps in front of the bullet meant for Link; or Claude, whose sense of loyalty we are forced to respect, thus qualifying our relationship with Link; but also 'that old man', the resolutely evil Dock Tobin himself. Lee J. Cobb's liking for the grandiose for once served a director well, and through him Mann was able to create his greatest character in the figure of the demented and totally corrupt old bandit frozen in time. The extent of the character's depravity comes through with an almost horrific force where Link and Dock face each other after all those years, and we learn what kind of past our apparently timid hero has had. Mann gives the scene in the old shack a black, oppressive atmosphere, Cooper standing silent and powerless surrounded by the grotesques, Trout, Coaley, Ponch, as his stepfather greets him: 'You been eating good? . . . you ran out and left me . . . I put a piece of work into you . . . you were my property . . . do you remember Uvalde? . . . eleven thousand dollars . . . you held him, I took off the top of his head . . . I could have pushed your guts through your back . . . every idea in your head . . . look at these pigs . . . there's no guts any more . . . NO GUTS!'

The end of the film sustains the strange honour that grows up round Tobin. With all of his 'sons' dead by Link (one of their number), having himself raped Billie as he must since she functions in the action as Link's woman, with the knowledge somewhere in his demented brain that Lassoo ('It rings in my head – Lassooo!') is no longer a thriving mining town his for the picking but, like Dock Tobin, a ghost – he stands atop his lonely mountain, a figure of tragic force, and watches his son – caught in an equally tragic situation – come to kill him. There is an unforgivable, absurd line from Cooper – 'I'm gonna take you in' – corrected immediately by an exchange that crystallizes the dilemmas of the two men: Link wildly rushing up the incline: 'You've outlived your time'; Dock lumbering wildly down from the crest: 'Kill me . . . you've lost your taste for it.' Integrity intact to the end, Tobin forces his stepson to destroy him, firing widely and continuing the demented soliloquy that is his basic mode of expression, until he is finally silenced.

Throughout the film Mann creates a complex sense of tragic inevitability, by his care with Dock and Claude communicating to us their awareness, brought home to them by Link, of themselves as anachronisms, and consequently of Link as their fate; this in turn balanced by Link's growing awareness, Hamlet-like, of what he must do. This awareness is strongest where the brothers, Link and Claude, finally resolve the issues between them in the landscape of the past, the ghost town of Lassoo. A *tour de force* by Mann, the scene, beginning with Claude's 'I want to see you, Cousin', and Link's response 'Over here, Cousin', is shot with immense authority, the scope frame following and containing all the action, culminating in the classically pure shot of the two brothers above and below the porch of the worn-out bank, both wounded bloodily, Claude shouting, hysteria in his voice, 'You have to come to me', Link answering, 'It finishes here, what you've always wanted.'

Mann's evocation of evil in the film is extraordinary: even the moon at one point seems to glower. Tobin's gang is a marvellous assortment of gargoyles: the mute Trout, played as a crazed child by Royal Dano, who is allowed his two pitiable howls as he runs to die on the outskirts of Lassoo; the wolfish Coaley; Robert J. Wilke's dumb oaf, Ponch. John Dehner's more rational Claude rightly stands outside and above these Shakespearian appetites and buffoons. But over all presides Dock. When the main title of the film appears, the scope frame balances it against Cooper astride his horse like a statue. But this is one of Mann's deceptions: the film itself leaves little doubt over who is the man of the West.

Mann's response to the western was not a response to history, as with Ford and Peckinpah, but to its archetypal form, the mythic patterns deeply imbedded in the plots and characters of the genre that can shape and structure the action. Although little interested in the simple oppositions of the traditional western romance, it was precisely these elements which allowed Mann to turn the genre to his purpose, hero and villain transmuted into protagonist and antagonist. Mann's fascination with the superior, charismatic individual found a rich outlet in the form, if no easy solution. The hero, his sanity at stake, enters the world of ordinary mortals only through a kind of metaphysical suicide, destroying the mirror of his magic, the incarnation of his pride and ambition. The villain finds his release only through madness and death.

The Community

For Mann the community is the family. It is this equation that accounts for the hero's ambiguous status on the edges of the society, the passion and power of the character, the private and violent nature of his struggle. This is clearest in *Winchester '73* where the theme of the family organizes and sharpens the action, although the episodic movement ensures some diffuseness. Dodge City, where the brothers compete for the rifle, is created by Mann as a homey place with children much in evidence ruled over by a fatherly Wyatt Earp. Thereafter, the action moves with the Winchester as it passes from Dutch to a gun-runner to the Indian chief, Young Bull, who promptly trains it on the young couple Steve and Lola, travelling to look at a possible home for themselves once they marry. Seemingly irrelevant in the movement of the film, the couple are central to its action, the tawdry Lola and the cowardly Steve both trying to find roles within the society by becoming a family unit. This structure is extended by Mann's treatment of the troopers in the besieged camp whom he creates as a group of young boys away from home under the guidance of Jay C. Flippen's fatherly sergeant-major. Here in one of Mann's finest scenes, before the dawn attack of the Indians, all the characters speak to the theme of putting down roots, building a family, having a home. The structure is finally rounded out by Waco, who dashes Lola's hopes by killing Steve and terrorizes a family with whom he takes cover, their homestead burnt to the ground as a result. Waco is a usurper and stands with Dutch, who in killing his father has left the community irrevocably; Mann places the character in sharp opposition to 'people' by having him caricature normal relationships, casting Steve in the role of house-wife, brutalizing Lola by imposing a grotesque love relationship on her.

Waco dies, appropriately, in the main street of town. But Lin and Dutch confront each other, as they must, in the brutal landscape outside the community. The central paradox in Mann is that although the values of the community are always at stake, the community itself is powerless, its forms and institutions inadequate to the threat. This perhaps accounts for the pathetic figures of Steve and Lola, their incarnation of an ideal at its weakest; Mann himself might have said he was only being realistic. Certainly, the consistency of his treatment of the community throughout all the films is remarkable. Typically children, old people and adolescent, sexless girls, the social order is always highly vulnerable and easily corrupted. In *The Far Country*, for instance, Dawson is a marvellous collection of old wrecks. Mann treats the citizenry with real affection, giving the old cronies, Ben and Luke, a moral awareness and stature, creating Hominy and Grits, the spinsters who run the restaurant, as warm, tough human beings. Here, as with the community elder played by Jay C. Flippen in *Bend of the River*, a variation of the patriarch who often accompanies the hero, Mann nicely communicates the tenacious, enduring qualities of the community. But as the action of the films always makes clear, these qualities are essentially helpless when faced with naked power.

At his most pessimistic Mann suggests that the community exiles or destroys its best features, anarchy and evil disguised as order forcing out reason and humanity. This idea is clear in *Devil's Doorway*, where the ending suggests that the society is committing suicide. Similarly, *The Tin Star* demonstrates how the community brings about the death of its very soul – the saintly Doc McCord – by denying the existence of evil which its own attitudes create. This is of course the dialectic at work behind the bounty hunter, a figure Mann clearly found fascinating. Mann must have responded to the tragic potential of the situation: the hero thrown from the heavenly community like a Miltonic angel to land, wounded and bitter, in some hellish landscape. 'Evil be *thou* my good.' Scratch many Mann heroes, in fact, and you find something akin to the sensibility of the bounty hunter. The process of alienation was described with great force by Mann in *The Last Frontier*, like *Devil's Doorway* a film that makes a frontal attack on the values of society. Mann tempts us into tight identification with

The Last Frontier: Jed, Mungo and Gus in the army camp

his comically frank, uncluttered hero and consequently compels us to experience the community as he does, as an irrational, suicidal world. A civilized man can jeopardize a whole community, can order a murder through an intermediary. But simply to kill a man, face to face, even though he is a canker within the society, is the act of an animal. For a man simply to take a woman, destructively joined to another, because he loves her – this too is not correct. What defeats Jed finally is the idealism of society, its insistence on theory and chivalry in the face of evil. For the unnatural passion of a Marston the society has traditional modes of expression; but the purity of a Cooper must be destroyed before he can enter the community. In such a world, the pragmatic, empirical man, the physical, visceral style – these are lost.

Mann's vision of the family as microcosm of humanity is profoundly ambiguous: the highest good, the source of all evil. Working within the western Mann over the years was able to clarify and shape his area of interest, inevitably seizing on the tragic and epic potential of the theme: the modest *Winchester '73*, inherited by Mann in 1950 when Fritz Lang left the project, extended into the grand designs of *The Man from Laramie* in 1955 (*God's Little Acre* coming in 1957), *Man of the West* in 1958, and culminating with the mutilated *Cimarron* in 1960, Mann naturally moving thereafter into the full-scale epics of the Cid and Rome. Relevant to all of these works is the theme of usurpation, the cosmic conflicts of dynasty that are at the centre of Classical tragedy. This is perhaps most prominent in *The Man from Laramie*, Mann and his script-writer Philip Yordan clearly attempting a loose reworking of *Oedipus Rex* within the genre. The structure of the film places the roots of the evil many years back, in Waggoman's passing over the woman he loved – the tough, tired Kate who still waits for him – to marry a wealthy Eastern woman instead. This unnatural act had resulted in their one son, Dave, taking on not only Alec's tragic flaw of ambition but a feminine weakness as well. The evil spreads, the ambitious Vic repeating his stepfather's pattern in his relationship with Barbara Waggoman. The fateful figure of Lockhart, reminding the old man of the furies that torture his nights, enters the scene to trigger the drama that must be played out. Inevitably, the only beloved son dies, the body brought home at dusk, the whole universe mourning with the king for his heir.

With *Man of the West* Mann returned directly to the terrain of *Winchester '73*, the hero driven tragically to preserve the ideal of the family by destroying its evil incarnation, redeeming the macrocosm by crucifying the microcosm, saving the world by giving himself. The charge provided by the archetypal cycle at the heart of all myth, the death and rebirth of the hero, always in evidence with Mann's work, is particularly strong here. But in *Cimarron*, adapted by Arnold Schulman from Edna Ferber's novel, Mann had material that while offering an epic theme was to prove less tractable in terms of his own interests. Inevitably, the film has a profound ambiguity at its centre, since the epic design demanded that Yancey be married (the only Mann hero of the westerns to be so, visibly, and consequently much less on the margins), while also carrying the incorrigible questing drive of a free spirit. The result is that *Cimarron* veers in tone from national epic to domestic drama, the marriage between Maria Schell and Glenn Ford frequently recalling the tense Stewart/Allyson relationships of *The Glenn Miller Story* and *Strategic Air Command.* An ironic paradox, rather than a tragic dilemma, emerges: the community is created and defended by the individual finally too foot-loose to stay within it.

Mann's tendency was always to work towards the heightened drama of family relationships: he bemoaned the lack of courage in producers who would not allow him to make Lockhart still another son to Waggoman, Billie the wife of Link. Thus the almost unholy force of that modest production, *The Naked Spur*, stems in part from the resemblance of the five characters to a malignant family bent on murdering each other at the first opportunity. Mann gives Janet Leigh's Lina the quality of a waif tagging along behind an older brother who fills the shoes of her dead outlaw pa. Ben functions generally as the eldest, evil son serenely above the struggles of Howie and Roy, yet inevitably determining the direction in which they move. A querulous old grandad to all of these, Millard Mitchell's Jesse fills out the structure.

By creating these relationships in the context of a parable, the situation drawing on at least two ancient and powerful myths, Christ in the wilderness and the theme of the rewards of acquisitiveness embodied in the classical situation of three men squabbling over gold, the whole held together by the journey structure (always central in Mann because of the pattern of death and resurrection it implies), Mann achieves an extraordinary intensity. The complex of associations gathers round the characters, Ben functioning at once as the gold that creates the destructive divisions among the other three and as a more personal temptation for Howie, the devil to his tortured Christ. Bent on destroying himself, Kemp swings violently from still moments with Lina to his more obsessive posture, unable to trust, to lean on anyone. The great power of the ending of the film is its unrelenting toughness, Howie still refusing

63

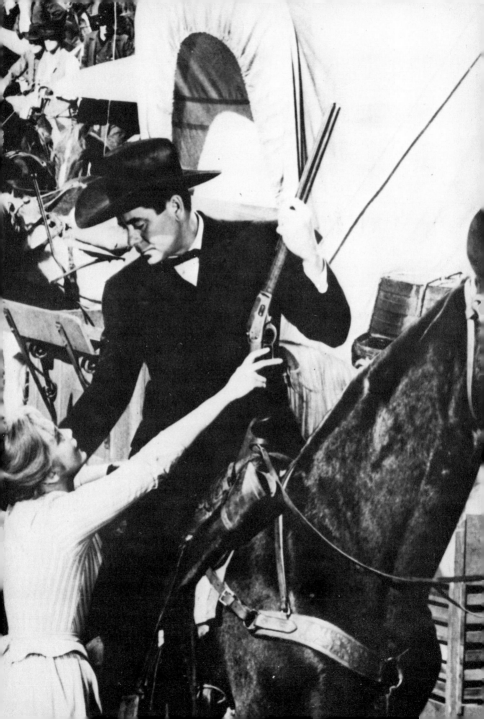

to recognize that Lina is the Holy Grail, not the gold of Ben's body, despite the evidence of three ugly deaths. Lina begging Howie to leave the corpse is beaten down, accepting that she will marry him whatever he does. 'But *why* . . . tell me *why*? I'm gonna sell him for *money*.' Finally unable to become inhuman, Kemp collapses against his saddle and cries.

The typical structure in Mann's films presents a spectrum of character ranging from representatives of the social order, highly rational and humane, through to the crazed and evil opposition. The hero stands at the centre torn between the two worlds. What makes his tragic struggles to rise above himself so credible is the fragility, the dependency, and the blindness, often damaging, of those values he is called upon to defend. Reason, humanity, democracy, these may be virtues; they are not necessarily power. There is an overwhelming feeling in Mann that nice guys always finish last. The knowledge of this makes Mann's heroes the neurotic men they are, accepting the role and responsibilities of being a nice guy with the greatest reluctance.

Landscape

A western is a wonderful thing to do because you take a group of actors who have acted on the stage or who have acted in rooms and now you take them out into the elements, and you throw them against the elements and the elements make them much greater as actors than if they were in a room. Because they have to shout above the winds, they have to suffer, they have to climb mountains . . .

For Mann all the West is a stage, but especially its mountains, streams and forests. The agrarian ideal, so central to Ford, has little relevance for Mann's work: the fecund valley, the frontier homestead – these are largely absent. Mann's West is the wilderness, 'way up in that far country' where the passions he deals with can find expression, his conflicts their resolutions. It is in the name of furrowed earth and a world where neighbours are possible that his characters finally act: but the universe they inhabit is one of rushing rivers and the lonely, brutal rocks of the snowline.

If Mann's cinema is pre-eminently a cinema of landscape, it is because through landscape he communicates a view of life. For Mann space is concrete and continuous, shaping action and

The Naked Spur: the rocks

determining outcome. On a minor key, for example, it is striking how in *Bend of the River* Mann creates the sense of a community on the move and blending with the terrain. Mann's sketch of the community putting down roots is only that, brief images of land being cleared, over which we hear Jay C. Flippen's commentary – surprisingly, given Mann's commitment to pictorial values. These are more characteristically in evidence in the fine scene where the river boat can go no further, the men slowly transporting the supplies through shallow water on to the beach. The architectural sense informing the use of location and colour is impressive, the scene caught carefully in long-shot, the eye driven through space from the shore along the line of porters back to the *River Queen*.

Scenes of action in Mann always take on force by being set in locations so that we have a sense, *physically*, of what is going on. Small details sharpen this, the rock-slides at the outset of *The Naked Spur*, like Ben's ugly target practice on the dead Jesse's boots at the end, increasing our awareness of the situation. Always we are given a tactical understanding and therefore a greater involvement with the action. It is this principle that informs the great care that Mann takes in setting up the ambush of the Blackfeet. As Kemp's party approach a small glade the deep-focus shot reveals the Indians in the distance cresting a small hill on the trail and disappearing from view. Moments later the Blackfeet gallop in to rein up as Howie and Lina, Ben and Jesse, slowly move across, Mann cutting from close-ups of the nervous faces back to the Indians, and then panning from the side of the trail with the group so that as they pass us and approach the forest's edge we see Roy buried in the shrubbery, rifle to hand. The bounty hunter's party pull up, turning, and now the Blackfeet move peacefully through the clearing, Mann repeating the pan so that our vantage-point is again Roy's as they pass to be caught in the middle, his hail of fire behind, Kemp's party ahead. The massacre, shattering for us in its efficiency, in retrospect appears inevitable.

But at a deeper level, Mann's landscape provides a correlative for the drive and conflict of his characters. The physicality of

The Naked Spur: the torrent

Mann's style creates a world that is hard and punishing towards moral disorder, unnatural, extreme behaviour. Justice emerges not from within the individual soul or through a social dialectic: standing outside and above man there exists a cosmic equilibrium, a natural law which demands a paying of dues. This is the meaning of the rushing torrents at the end of both *Bend of the River* and *The Naked Spur*, the swirling rivers of an immutable justice that spirit away the vice of an Emerson Cole, a Roy Anderson. In *The Man from Laramie* the cache of rifles is at the lip of a spur, accessible only by a steep ascent doubling back on itself along the cliff-face. During the film we watch all the characters pit themselves and their horses against the terrain, driving precariously against space and ground to achieve their desperate ends. The spur dominates in the resolution of the action, Dave dying at its crest by his stepbrother's hand, Vic savaged by the Apache near its base, the buckboard of rifles forced over the lip by Lockhart to hurtle to their destruction below. But a key moment is the slow yet relentless ascent of Alec Waggoman up the tortuous path which culminates in the frenzied Vic being driven to push the blind old man over the edge. Ironic, terrible, but finally liberating, the act lays bare the evil, Waggoman dying and reborn through his fall.

The Far Country also takes on force through Mann's use of landscape to evoke a universal justice. 'It can do things to a man – make him crazy. . . .' Luke's paean to gold is interrupted by the roar of the avalanche of snow that sweeps down from the heights of White Pass across the mountain trail, an awesome assertion of natural forces that brings low the self-willed Ronda who has parted company with Jeff's group, driven by her haste over (rather than round) the icy slope. Jeff's solipsistic drive to leave Dawson to Gannon's tyrrany invites a similar intervention by fate. The two men, Ben complaining about having to travel to Juneau by raft to avoid Gannon, unpack their goods at river's edge, the surrounding forest and hill-side crowding them closely. Seconds later Ben is dead and Jeff has had his comeuppance, the result, as with Ronda, of an anonymous and implacable attack from on high.

Where the traditional imagery of the western intersected with Mann's preoccupations, offering an image through which he could express and focus his themes, was in the recurrent visual motif of a man alone in landscape. But for Mann the landscape was specific, the man, time and again, on a *mountain*. Great height is always important in Mann, a clue to the reach and conflict of his characters on the one hand, the transcendent forces of justice which they defy on the other. In a superficial way, the scene in *Bend of the River* where Glyn, Cole and Trey fire down from a cliff pocket on to their pursuers works to differentiate the three men, Glyn easing off once the attack is broken, Cole firing on with relish, Trey asking why stop? But the real force in the scene stems directly from our sense of how exact and cruel the justice is that is being visited on the greedy townsmen below. Study of the topography of *Bend of the River* repays itself, illuminating the deceptive movement of the film in which Cole, by his act of defying the community – leaving his better impulses in the form of the savagely beaten

McLyntock to perish atop snowy Mount Hood – becomes a tragic figure. The hero in turn becomes an omnipotent force firing down from high up in the terrain, blocking Cole's every step. Creating him only as gunfire, movement and a voice in the landscape, Mann suggests the spirit of an implacable justice working itself out through the figure of McLyntock.

Occasionally, Mann heightens the action by an ironic use of landscape. Hence the openness of the range Will Lockhart covers as he rounds up Kate's strays, the great plain stained moments later by Dave Waggoman's evil act, blowing a bullet through the hand of the incredulous hero. The scene recalls an earlier moment, and one of Mann's most impressive uses of space and terrain, where Lockhart and his men are quietly loading their wagons on the edge of a sprawling sea of salt. A large body of riders appear, a far-off speck in the distance, as the men work on in the tranquil sunshine. Mann holds the shot an audaciously long time, its depth of field ensuring a gradual build-up of foreboding as the group slowly make ground at a dead run round the curve of the salt flats towards Lockhart, Mann finally releasing the tension, panning hard with the dark riders as they thunder past on the ridge over-head to rein up. Mann's control over the changing tone of the scene is total, arming us with a suspicion of the violence that may occur only to disarm us – as Lockhart himself is disarmed – by the hysteria of what does follow.

But more typically, Mann exercises the expressive potential of the medium to create a *pathetic* relationship between man and environment, inevitable given his view of the protagonist as micro-cosm of humanity, social order and justice as attributes of natural law. Thus in the opening scene of *The Man from Laramie* the landscape seems to brood over Lockhart as he explores the setting of his brother's death. The scope image – Mann's first and strik-ingly assured use of the wide screen – is filled completely by the crater in which the silent hero stands, the lip of the terrain behind curling round and above the solitary figure bitterly fingering a dusty cavalry-man's hat in the growing twilight. Structurally, the treatment of the moment is particularly important, since it looks forward to the later scene where the body of Dave is brought home, the dark images supported by a moaning chorus, the last act of the drama beginning with Alec Waggoman now cast in Lockhart's role.

At its most dynamic Mann's style takes on an expressionist edge, resulting from his unremitting concentration on interior conflict. Rarely articulated, the action characteristically flows below the surface to break out in strangely malignant scenes of great physical intensity. It is this subterranean drive that gives much of Mann's work a static, disembodied quality, as if a private obsession were at work on the material rather than being disciplined and put at its service. At times Mann's cinema reaches an electrifying pitch in the relentless way it focuses on the unnatural struggle of extreme men, trapped in the ugly, unyielding rocks of a horrific landscape. One of the great pleasures of *Winchester '73* is that the nervy contest for the rifle with which the film opens is only a play, a parody of what must happen but cannot here, since the passions at work are contained by the community. Only away from 'people' – in the private world of open space – can the cataclysmic release of those deep, violent drives take place, civil strife between brother and brother, men from the same womb filled with hatred, sacred family blood being redeemed. Mann's treatment of the final confrontation in *Winchester '73* gives it a concrete quality, the wind whipping over the brothers as they try in turn to bury each other in the brutal rocks, the punishing, merciless pressure of the rifleshots shattering the air and throwing up a choking dust. This physical intensity, together with the ritualistic exchanges of the two men over their father as they fire, gives the scene a force that mounts to a psychic peak. The terrain is so coloured by the action that it finally seems an inner landscape, the unnatural world of a disturbed mind.

Dramatic Structure and Style

Well of course violence is a very strange thing. If you follow all the great plays, whether they're Greek, Shakespearian . . . heads roll. Most gruesome . . . even in King Lear *when they jab Gloucester's eyes out with the spurs. I haven't done that yet, I use the spur, though, the naked spur for a weapon. But actually this is true of great drama, that it needs violence because the audience is sitting there and they are*

Winchester '73: the shooting contest

experiencing things, and then in order for it to take hold the dramatist really needs . . . to express an emotion, for the character to go through something that the audience feel for.

The Mann hero functions as a *scapegoat.* The scenes of greatest force in Mann are always where violence smites the hero who, like Job, seems to have done little to deserve it. Will Lockhart, the least ambiguous of Mann's revenge protagonists, suffers most. Where Kemp, Webster and Hickman have turned their backs on the world, and where McAdam, McLyntock and Jones turn on their own kin or kind, Lockhart is a more familiar figure, seeking the revenge of a brother whose death derives from the act of strangers. Yet the revenge drive, which normally requires no validation within the genre, vibrates in Mann with primeval significance, operating as a flaw in the hero who is seen to raise himself up and presume to judge. As the action of the films makes clear, this form of *hubris* is tantamount to self-destruction, the impulse embodied in the

Bend of the River: the hero undergoes a test

sudden, unnatural violence the hero both expresses and suffers in the course of his struggle. A cosmic revenge is visited upon the revenger. Lockhart, roped and dragged through a fire, must watch helplessly as his wagons are burnt and his innocent mules destroyed, must stand, pitiable and horrified, as a bullet is shot through his hand. Very strong in all of Mann is the ritualistic idea of violence as a punishing test which the hero must be mercilessly exposed to and cleansed by. So McAdam must suffer the hail of bullets from his brother, McLyntock must be left bloody and alone atop his mountain, Owens must 'walk through the nettles' of his encounter with Bogardus. In cameo the idea is there in *Devil's Doorway* with Jimmy, the little Shoshone boy, passing his painful initiation test, returning from above the snowline with the claws of an eagle. For Mann we learn only through suffering, experience and environment bending and beating us into shape. Education – life itself – is pain.

This tragic pattern is the core of Mann's art. The punishment that the hero sustains in his obsessive pursuit of a villain who is a projection of himself is in turn visited upon us; for we have projected ourselves into the hero. Mann had come to Hollywood from Broadway; with him he brought a sure knowledge of the importance of a pure line of narrative action and a dramatic structure that evokes a both personal and universal conflict. If the dialectics of tragedy are not wholly realized, if we do not emerge from a Mann movie having experienced horror and pity and having finally been cleansed, it is not because Mann did not try. Like Hitchcock, Mann puts us through it, forcing upon us a relationship with the hero despite unsettling doubts, then finally smiting us – and the protagonist – from his position, god-like, outside and above the action. If the morality is an overweening one, the understanding of medium and audience is impressive.

The hall-mark of Mann's style is a mobile camera, moving fluidly with the action, its pace and direction dictated by the drive of the character. Will Lockhart steps off from Barbara Waggoman's store in a barely controlled, infinitely determined march towards the corral and Dave some distance off, the camera receding smoothly before him, the intensity of its concentration and the relentlessness of its retreat creating the meaning for us. The style, always evoking a sense of the continuity and physicality of space, is also marked by the close-up, evidence of Mann's commitment to passion and an expressive cinema. 'Look at it!' screams Dave, brandishing his bleeding palm in Lockhart's face, the hero held fast by two Barb cowboys. The camera moves down to Lockhart's quivering hand, Dave stripping away the glove, the gun poised and cocked – and then glides upward with the explosion to a tight shot on the violated, ashen face. Mann's cinema has often been seen as a notoriously violent one: it is therefore odd how little, relatively speaking, violent *action* there is. The secret, as all the old Hollywood veterans seem to know (see *Psycho* or *Rio Bravo*), is to allow the whole to be coloured by one or two parts. Thus much of the violence in Mann is a violence of atmosphere, not a blow struck or a gun fired in what is arguably his most arresting moment, the first

The Tin Star: the frame as a stage within which the action can be played

meeting of the brothers in *Winchester '73*. What both men *know* – that their guns hang in Earp's office – is gone in the frenzy of the moment, the brothers simultaneously slapping leather with electric speed. The image of Stewart, his face ablaze, fairly quivers with murderous intent.

Mann naturally shies away from cutting for his effects, treating the frame itself as a stage within which the action can be played out. The recurrent use of deep focus enhances the effect, the eye drawn into the situation to locate the key elements of the drama. As Lin grapples with a villain on the sidewalk, across the street the bank is being robbed by Dutch, Mann sharply extending the suspense in us by forcing us to look through a violently bucking stagecoach in front of the saloon in an effort to spot the brother. The world created is a morally ambiguous one, protagonist and antagonist balanced on the same plane of action. Time and again two men – always two men – held tightly within the frame savage each other in a river, a dark cave, under the hooves of horses: in *Man of the West* the horizontal line of the porch divides the image cleanly, Link above, Claude below.

A rich contrast to John Ford in many ways, Mann followed the old veteran in the common cause of a visual cinema, pictorial values above all. The kinds of conflict and the terrain itself are vastly different, but the style in both cases unfailingly roots the action in the sweep and pull of landscape. For Ford this broader canvas provided the structure through which he could express his poetic vision of America, in the process carrying on almost single-handedly the romantic mainstream tradition of the genre. For Mann space was cosmic, the camera ever standing back to place his characters in a continuous and elemental reality, Prometheuses chained to their rocks. His contribution was in its way equally unique, the incarnation of his tragic world darkening the genre as no one else has. His neurotic characters and their extraordinary violence were a strange personal gift to the western, extending its frontiers for both audience and film-makers that were to follow. The sensibility at work was a peculiar one: highly modern in its preoccupation with psychology and violence; oddly anachronistic in its fascination with the austere morality and art of Classical Greece and Elizabethan England. Remarkably, the western allowed the welding of these elements and the expression of Mann's own troubled dialectic surrounding the individual and the cosmos.

Last Years

What is learning anything? It is doing something, however tawdry it may be. I've made some tawdry films, I've made some fair films, I've made, I think, a few good films . . . but all of it was a process of learning.

Few directors could have moved to the epic with surer credentials than Anthony Mann. In its way the step was to prove as momentous for him as his coming to the western, resulting in a great triumph, *El Cid* acclaimed everywhere, the most crushing of defeats, *The Fall of the Roman Empire* roundly condemned by all. Yet the two films are less black and white than that (except thematically), the vigour of the first balanced by the discipline of the second. Few of his generation, responding to the pressure of Hollywood's confused commercial climate of the late fifties, weathered the transition to the epic so well.

With the form Mann seemed at last to have arrived at ground he had been moving towards throughout his career. Apart from the archetypal conflicts that structured the films, there was an unheralded opportunity to focus on key ritualistic situations – the joust, torture by fire – against the back-drop of epic landscape. Mann seized on the potential, scenes such as the exhausting swordfight of the challengers and the resurrection of the Cid, the punishing test of faith undergone by James Mason's Greek philosopher-slave and Marcus Aurelius' sombre funeral in the falling snow, moments of memorable quality. Yet although the achievement of these works is considerable, neither film has the consistency and power that his work within the western had achieved. It may be that Mann did as well as he could given the size and demands of the form. But finally there lurks the suspicion that Mann was always at his best where the narrative structure threw up models that allowed for archetypal extension, rather than the particularized situations themselves: *The Naked Spur* or *Man of the West* rather than *Hamlet*. It was in *reaching* that Mann became alive, impregnating his material, frequently tired and worn, with passionate meanings. Getting there Mann may have discovered he had little to say.

Either way, Mann withdrew into silence. *The Heroes of Telemark*, Mann's final, ravishing tribute to the snowline and his *hommage* to the silent cinema, was a slender work. Centring on the old themes of the costs of being human and the emotional education of the hero – here compelled to move away from the rational posture that he shares with the Nazis – the action is somewhat mechanically followed through, finally dwarfed by the beautiful silent scenes of warfare in the majestic white Norwegian landscape. *A Dandy in Aspic*, Mann's last film, the veteran dying in the final stages of shooting, achieved snatches of intensity despite the restrictions of an urban setting. Here Mann returned, perhaps appropriately, to *T-Man* territory and the counterpoint of character of the westerns,

El Cid; The Heroes of Telemark

building it round a new version of his hero, a tired Russian double-agent anxious about his identity, reaching out to feel, hopeful of escape from a ruthless past and a Cold War world of power. The structure is embodied in the opposition of the hero, Eberlin, to Gaddis, the British agent, a mechanical, emotionless man. Ordered by the British to murder himself – in his Russian *persona* – Eberlin finally does so, shooting Gaddis and thus destroying his past even as it destroys him, Gaddis's car running him over on the airport tarmac.

When he died Mann was planning *The King*, a reworking of *King Lear* set in the West. Mann seems always to have worked at an intuitive level – both his career and the films are a hymn to American pragmatism – and he may have come to feel that in returning to the form he might recover the drive and direction of earlier periods. Certainly it is difficult to escape the view that in the sixties Mann had lost his way. In a sense it could be said that with the epic Mann had used himself up, not only exhausting appropriate forms but his themes as well. There is a desperation about Mann's embracing of the emerging genre of the spy movie, as if a sense of his irrelevance to the contemporary context had been borne in on him. Yet Mann was always to be a prisoner of his empiricism. Despite the shifts of form and subject there is finally a compulsive, strangely static quality about Mann's career, a lack of growth and development that, perhaps inevitably, parallels the action of many of the individual films. Like his heroes, Mann can be seen to have tested himself all his artistic life; yet the disturbing questions that can both cripple a career and open new vistas may never have been faced, perhaps could not be posed. But for a time Mann had touched the heights: his place is assured.

Filmography: Anthony Mann

Born 1906 in San Diego, California (real name Emil Bundsmann). Died 1967.
Mann began in the theatre, as an actor at the Triangle Theatre, Greenwich
Village, New York. He directed several plays in New York, including *Thunder
on the Left*, *Cherokee Night* (by Lynn Riggs), *The Big Blow* (by Theodore Pratt)
and *So Proudly We Hail*. In 1938 he was signed by Selznick as casting director
and talent scout, and supervised screen tests for *The Young in Heart* (Richard
Wallace, 1938), *Intermezzo* (Gregory Ratoff, 1939), *Gone With the Wind* (Victor
Fleming, 1939), *Rebecca* (Alfred Hitchcock, 1940), and several other films. He
was assistant to Preston Sturges on *Sullivan's Travels* (1941), and story-writer
on Richard Fleischer's *Follow Me Quietly* (1949), with Francis Rosenwald.

Features

1942 *Dr Broadway, Moonlight in Havana*
1943 *Nobody's Darling*
1944 *My Best Gal, Strangers in the Night*
1945 *The Great Flamarion, Two O'Clock Courage, Sing Your Way Home*
1946 *Strange Impersonation, The Bamboo Blonde*
1947 *Desperate* (also story, with Dorothy Atlas), *Railroaded, T-Men* (also script,
uncredited, with John C. Higgins)
1948 *Raw Deal*
1949 *Reign of Terror, Border Incident, Side Street*
1950 *Devil's Doorway, Winchester '73, The Furies*
1951 (*Quo Vadis*) (Director Mervyn LeRoy. Mann directed the Fire of Rome
sequences), *The Tall Target*
1952 *Bend of the River* (British title: *Where the River Bends*), *The Naked Spur*
1953 *Thunder Bay*
1954 *The Glenn Miller Story, The Far Country*
1955 *Strategic Air Command, The Man From Laramie, The Last Frontier*
1956 *Serenade, Men in War*
1957 *The Tin Star, God's Little Acre* (also produced, with Sidney Harmon)

1958 *Man of the West*
1960 *Cimarron*
1961 *El Cid*
1964 *The Fall of the Roman Empire*
1965 *The Heroes of Telemark* (in Great Britain)
1967 *A Dandy in Aspic* (in Great Britain) (also produced. Completed by
  Laurence Harvey after Mann's death)

Westerns
Devil's Doorway (1950)

Production Company	M.G.M.
Producer	Nicholas Nayfack
Director	Anthony Mann
Script	Guy Trosper
Director of Photography	John Alton
Editor	Conrad Nervig
Art Directors	Cedric Gibbons, Leonard Vasian
Music	Daniele Amfitheatrof

Robert Taylor (*Lance Poole*), Louis Calhern (*Verne Coolan*), Paula Raymond
(*Orrie Masters*), Marshall Thompson (*Rod MacDougall*), James Mitchell (*Red
Rock*), Edgar Buchanan (*Zeke Carmody*), Spring Byington (*Mrs Masters*).

Running time: 83 mins.
Distributor: M.G.M.

Winchester '73 (1950)

Production Company	Universal-International
Producer	Aaron Rosenberg
Director	Anthony Mann
Script	Robert L. Richards and Borden Chase, from a story by Stuart N. Lake
Director of Photography	William Daniels
Editor	Edward Curtiss
Art Directors	Bernard Herzbrun and Nathan Juran
Music Director	Joseph Gershenson

James Stewart (*Lin McAdam*), Shelley Winters (*Lola Manners*), Dan Duryea
(*Waco Johnnie Dean*), Stephen McNally (*Dutch Henry Brown*), Millard Mitchell
(*High Spade*), Charles Drake (*Steve Miller*), John McIntyre (*Joe Lamont*), Will
Geer (*Wyatt Earp*), Jay C. Flippen (*Sgt Wilkes*), Rock Hudson (*Young Bull*).

Running time: 92 mins.
Distributor: G.F.D.

The Furies (1950)

Production Company	Paramount
Producer	Hal B. Wallis
Director	Anthony Mann
Script	Charles Schnee, from the novel by Niven Busch
Director of Photography	Victor Milner
Editor	Archie Marshek
Art Directors	Hans Dreier and Henry Bumstead
Music	Franz Waxman

Barbara Stanwyck (*Vance Jeffords*), Walter Huston (*T. C. Jeffords*), Wendell Corey (*Rip Darrow*), Judith Anderson (*Flo Burnett*), Gilbert Roland (*Juan*), Thomas Gomez (*El Tigre*), Beulah Bondi (*Mrs Annaheim*), Wallace Ford (*Hyslip*), Albert Dekker (*Mr Reynolds*), Blanche Yurka (*Herrera Mother*).

Running time: 109 mins.
Distributor: Paramount.

Bend of the River (1952)

Production Company	Universal-International
Producer	Aaron Rosenberg
Director	Anthony Mann
Script	Borden Chase
Director of Photography	Irving Glassberg
Colour Process	Technicolor
Editor	Russell Schoengarth
Art Directors	Bernard Herzbrun, Nathan Juran
Music	Hans J. Salter

James Stewart (*Glyn McLyntock*), Arthur Kennedy (*Emerson Cole*), Julia Adams (*Laura Baile*), Rock Hudson (*Trey Wilson*), Jay C. Flippen (*Jeremy Baile*), Stepin' Fetchit (*Adam*), Lori Nelson (*Marjie*), Henry Morgan (*Shorty*).

Running time: 91 mins.
Distributor: G.F.D.
British title WHERE THE RIVER BENDS.

The Naked Spur (1952)

Production Company	M.G.M.
Producer	William H. Wright
Director	Anthony Mann
Script	Sam Rolfe and Harold Jack Bloom
Director of Photography	William Mellor
Colour Process	Technicolor
Editor	George White

Art Directors	Cedric Gibbons, Malcolm Brown
Music	Bronislau Kaper

James Stewart (*Howard Kemp*), Robert Ryan (*Ben Vandergroat*), Janet Leigh (*Lina Patch*), Ralph Meeker (*Roy Anderson*), Millard Mitchell (*Jesse Tate*).

Running time: 91 mins.
Distributor: M.G.M.
First shown in Britain in 1953.

The Far Country (1954)

Production Company	Universal-International
Producer	Aaron Rosenberg
Director	Anthony Mann
Script	Borden Chase
Director of Photography	William Daniels
Colour Process	Technicolor
Editor	Russell Schoengarth
Art Directors	Bernard Herzbrun, Alex Golitzen
Music	Joseph Gershenson

James Stewart (*Jeff Webster*), Ruth Roman (*Ronda Castle*), Corinne Calvert (*Renée Vallon*), Walter Brennan (*Ben Tatem*), John McIntyre (*Mr Gannon*), Jay C. Flippen (*Rube*), Henry Morgan (*Ketchum*), Steve Brodie (*Ives*), Royal Dano (*Luke*).

Running time: 96 mins.
Distributor: G.F.D.

The Man from Laramie (1955)

Production Company	Columbia
Producer	William Goetz
Director	Anthony Mann
Script	Philip Yordan and Frank Burt, from a *Saturday Evening Post* story by Thomas T. Flynn
Director of Photography	Charles Lang (filmed in CinemaScope)
Colour Process	Technicolor
Editor	William Lyon
Art Director	Cary Odell
Music	George Duning
Song 'Man from Laramie' composed by	Leslie Lee and Ned Washington
Recording Supervisor	John Livadary
Sound	George Cooper

James Stewart (*Will Lockhart*), Arthur Kennedy (*Vic Hansbro*), Donald Crisp (*Alec Waggoman*), Cathy O'Donnell (*Barbara Waggoman*), Alex Nicol (*Dave Waggoman*), Aline MacMahon (*Kate Canaday*), Wallace Ford (*Charley O'Leary*),

Shooting *Man of the West:* Anthony Mann left of camera

Jack Elam (*Chris Boldt*), John War Eagle (*Frank Darrah*), James Millican (*Tom Quigby*).

Running time: 101 mins.
Distributor: Columbia.

The Last Frontier (1955)

Production Company	Columbia
Producer	William Fadiman
Director	Anthony Mann
Script	Philip Yordan and Russell S. Hughes, based on a novel by Richard Emery Roberts
Director of Photography	William Mellor (filmed in CinemaScope)
Colour Process	Technicolor
Editor	Al Clark
Art Director	Robert Peterson
Music	Leigh Harline
Song 'The Last Frontier' composed by	Lester Lee and Ned Washington
Sound	John Livadary

Victor Mature (*Jed Cooper*), James Whitmore (*Gus*), Robert Preston (*Colonel Marston*), Guy Madison (*Captain Riordan*), Anne Bancroft (*Corinna*), Peter Whitney (*Sgt Dekker*), Pat Hogan (*Mungo*).

Running time: 97 mins.
Distributor: Columbia.
First shown in Britain in 1956.

The Tin Star (1957)

Production Company	A Perlberg-Seaton Production
Producers	William Perlberg, George Seaton
Director	Anthony Mann
Script	Dudley Nichols
Story	Barney Slater, Joel Kane
Director of Photography	Loyal Griggs (filmed in VistaVision)
Editor	Alma Macrorie
Art Directors	Hal Pereira, Joseph MacMillan Johnson
Music	Elmer Bernstein

Henry Fonda (*Morg Hickman*), Anthony Perkins (*Ben Owens*), Betsy Palmer (*Nona Mayfield*), Michel Ray (*Kip*), Neville Brand (*Bart Bogardus*), John McIntyre (*Doc McCord*), Mary Webster (*Millie Parker*), Peter Baldwin (*Zeke McGaffey*) Lee Van Cleef (*Ed McGaffey*).

Running time: 93 mins.
Distributor: Paramount.

Man of the West (1958)

Production Company	Ashton Productions
Producer	Walter M. Mirisch
Director	Anthony Mann
Script	Reginald Rose, from a novel by Will C. Brown
Director of Photography	Ernest Haller (filmed in CinemaScope)
Colour Process	De Luxe
Editor	Richard Heermance
Art Director	Hilyard Brown
Sound	Jack Solomon
Music	Leigh Harline

Gary Cooper (*Link Jones*), Julie London (*Billie Ellis*), Lee J. Cobb (*Dock Tobin*), Arthur O'Connell (*Sam Beasley*), Jack Lord (*Coaley*), John Dehner (*Claude*), Royal Dano (*Trout*), Robert J. Wilke (*Ponch*), Jack Williams (*Alcutt*), Guy Wilkerson (*Conductor*), Chuck Robertson (*Rifleman*).

Running time: 95 mins.
Distributor: United Artists.
First shown in Britain in 1959.

Cimarron (1960)

Production Company	M.G.M.
Producer	Edmund Grainger
Director	Anthony Mann
Script	Arnold Schulman. Based on Edna Ferber's novel
Director of Photography	Robert L. Surtees. Filmed in CinemaScope
Colour Process	Metrocolor
Editor	John Dunning
Art Directors	George W. Davis, Addison Hehr
Costumes	Walter Plunkett
Music	Frank Waxman
Title song composed by	Paul Francis Webster
sung by	The Roger Wagner Chorale
Special Effects	A. Arnold Gillespie, Lee LeBlanc, Robert R. Hoag
Sound	Franklin Milton

Glenn Ford (*Yancey Cravat*), Maria Schell (*Sabra Cravat*), Anne Baxter (*Dixie Lee*), Arthur O'Connell (*Tom Wyatt*), Russ Tamblyn (*The Cherokee Kid*), Mercedes McCambridge (*Sarah Wyatt*), Vic Morrow (*Wes*), Robert Keith (*Sam Pegler*), Charles McGraw (*Bob Yountis*), Henry (Harry) Morgan (*Jesse Rickey*), David Opatoshu (*Sol Levy*), Aline MacMahon (*Mrs Pegler*), Lili Darvas (*Felicia Venable*), Edgar Buchanan (*Neal Hefner*), Mary Wickes (*Mrs Hefner*), Royal Dano (*Ike Howes*), Vladimir Sokoloff (*Jacob Krubeckoff*).

Running time: 135 mins. Original running time: 140 mins.
Distributor: M.G.M.

3: Budd Boetticher: the Rules of the Game

Boetticher stands alone. There is much about this director's life and art that encourages this romantic notion. Where Ford, his roots deep in history, was to achieve a great respect within the industry; where Mann, sustained both by his experience of the stage and a natural empiricism, over the years collected three reputations (at home with the thriller, the western, the epic); Boetticher appears a diminutive and isolated figure working in the shadows, trying to create his art wholly out of himself. Often he has been likened to Hemingway, his work and career hovering between tragedy and cliché, only an unyielding integrity apparently forestalling the parody that his much-publicized individualism invites.

His bizarre entry into the world of movies as a bullfighter is now well known, Boetticher swapping his apprenticeship as a matador for a Hollywood career in 1941 when he was taken on as technical adviser for Mamoulian's *Blood and Sand*. Ten years later, after a string of small pictures, Boetticher shot what he has described as a largely autobiographical *The Bullfighter and the Lady*, John Ford assisting the John Wayne production by cutting the film and ensuring a prompt studio release. Always self-conscious, the director marked the film as a milestone by changing his credit from Oscar Boetticher, Jnr, to Budd. Yet the break-through was minor: if the contract with Universal that followed offered a base and more substantial performers, the production conditions for the

Randolph Scott in *The Tall T*

The Bullfighter and the Lady

adventure films and westerns that now occupied him remained cramping and unsympathetic.

In 1955 Boetticher had a second opportunity to undertake a personal project in *The Magnificent Matador*, easily his most ambitious production thus far. However, it was with the small western that followed this highly uneven work (and the taut thriller, *A Killer is Loose*) that Boetticher's career finally clicked. *Seven Men from Now* was the first of a brief cycle of westerns that were to emerge over the next four years. Highly successful commercially, these little films were to bring a measure of critical recognition in France, at least, where Bazin hailed *Seven Men from Now* as an 'exemplary western'. After a half-dozen of these, between each of which Boetticher was shooting footage for his long-cherished third bullfighting film, *Arruza*, the director went on to make *The Rise and Fall of Legs Diamond* in 1960. Then he left for Mexico to complete his project on the renowned matador, who was a close friend.

Astonishingly, the commitment to complete this personal production resulted in an eight-year exile before Boetticher was free to return, taking up his Hollywood career with another small western.

Hollywood and Mexico, bullfighting and the western, these are the polarities of Boetticher's world and point to the profound ambiguity at its centre. On the one hand there is the deepest commitment to a highly romantic individualism: life is seen as a solitary quest for meaning, an odyssey, action as a definition and expression of the self which is its own reward, compromise of personal integrity as indefensible. On the other hand there is Boetticher's chosen profession, the corporate and glossy public world of an industrial art, the Hollywood cinema, within which he was buried (his two original projects apart) for fifteen years. Perhaps only his competitive drive, the desire to do everything as well as possible, sustained him throughout this troubled, directionless period.

The contradictions inherent in Boetticher's position are clearest in his success. *Seven Men from Now* led directly to the Ranown cycle of westerns, all of which were produced by Harry Joe Brown (Boetticher himself was often associate producer), and which comprise the core of Boetticher's achievement thus far. All the films starred Randolph Scott, Brown's partner in the venture, and the more substantial works – *The Tall T*, *Ride Lonesome*, *Comanche Station* – were scripted by Burt Kennedy, whose first effort as a film-writer had been to adapt his western novella (of the same title) for *Seven Men from Now*. A reading of this story is instructive for any student of Boetticher's films: most of the situations, incidents and dialogue that were to be developed and refined in the cycle are already present here.

However, I am not suggesting that the films are not Boetticher's own. As Kennedy himself has pointed out, the scripts were as much Boetticher's as his; moreover, to examine the novels adapted by Charles Lang and Boetticher for *Decision at Sundown* and *Buchanan Rides Alone* is to recognize a pattern of meaningful changes (in particular, hero and villain being given a parallel stature) falling into place. With his own recent direction Kennedy has begun to reveal a sensibility far removed from the irony, discipline and stark confrontations of the Ranown cycle. While often quoting from the earlier scripts (sometimes in chunks), his work has tended to a broad comedy (often relaxing into vulgarity) which suggests the common ground that sustained this fertile collaboration. But in any case, if Boetticher's overall career has been a broken and artistically uneven one, the consistency of its thematic and formal preoccupations, from *The Bullfighter and the Lady* to *Arruza*, from *The Cimarron Kid* to *A Time for Dying*, seems undeniable.

Yet the Ranown cycle (my use of this term encompasses *Seven Men from Now*, which in fact was a Batjac production) was crucial to Boetticher in two ways. Firstly, it offered an enclave within the industry in which he could operate, a structure characterized less by studio bureaucracy than by the personal style of individuals who shared a common respect working together in a small outfit. While sheltering Boetticher from the destructive confrontations, the impulse to square off against the whole industry, that his individualist ethic exposes him to, this arrangement also offered him the opportunity to arrive at meaningful *form*. Boetticher's obsessive return to the subject of bullfighting is ample evidence of his belief in the validity of the matador, the ritualistic encounter with death providing action that is both personally and artistically meaningful. However, the completeness of the commitment to individualism, if privately sustaining, confines the film-maker: how dramatize a static world, action that is neither growth nor change? Here again Mann was the more fortunate, his heroes compulsively reaching out. Perhaps nothing testifies more eloquently to the flexibility of the western as an artistic model than the fact that it should have been so important in the development of two such disparate artists committed to starkly contrasting conceptions of character and dramatic action.

The sheer appeal of making westerns for Boetticher is obvious: like Ford he is a man of the outdoor life most at ease in good male company. As with Hawks, this extends into an ethic of physical action which is evident in the films; stunts and chases, careering buckboards and skirmishes with Indians, these are always shot

John Wayne, Randolph Scott and Budd Boetticher on the set of *Seven Men from Now*

with exuberance by Boetticher. But more importantly, at an ideological level the western is deeply attractive for Boetticher in its insistence on an archaic world where the ambiguous drama of individualism can be played out. Although not a man of the West like Peckinpah, Boetticher is fascinated by the idea of the frontier: it is this that explains his sojourns in Mexico, metaphorically speaking the last stronghold of the American West. However, the vulnerable men and women and the isolated swing stations that characterize Boetticher's frontier have little to do with history. Boetticher's West is quite simply *the world*, a philosophical ground over which his pilgrims move to be confronted with existential choices wholly abstracted from social contexts. Where Mann ever self-consciously edged the revenge western towards tragedy, Boetticher intuitively reversed the movement, gradually stripping the form of its revenge drive (and the metaphysical ethic it carries) to arrive at the structure of the morality play and the fable.

Unsupported by virtue, tradition or the community, Boetticher's characters confront their destiny nakedly. However, we are deceived if we consider them to be in control of it: sustained only by an idea of themselves in the fact of a mocking meaninglessness, the characters are helpless, doomed to play out their absurd roles in the tragi-comic game of life.

The Ranown cycle gave Boetticher a stable base and creative relationships which allowed him to refine his form, the films growing deeper and more personal until with *Ride Lonesome* and *Comanche Station* the controlled objectification of tensions, the appropriateness of form and style, approach perfection. But above all, Boetticher's westerns are a series, this director demonstrating more dramatically than most artists how understanding and appreciation of the single work can grow through a knowledge of earlier and later works. Moreover, Boetticher's achievement, although it is not inaccessible to all but the connoisseur, does require for its full impact an awareness of the fine adjustments he makes within the form. And this provides the final paradox. For if the Ranown team and the western gave Boetticher the latitude and structure through which he could create the ritualistic play that he finds meaningful, the results could never be fully satisfactory for the director. Boetticher's romanticism demanded of him that he rise above the industry and its genres rather than function there *mano á mano*, that single-handedly he create the *apocalyptical* work, the original masterpiece, his *magnum opus*. Living out the myth of his individualism to the hilt, Boetticher cut free from the constraints and disciplines of the industry to find himself, like his characters, moving through bewildering and dangerous experiences, a commitment to personal style finally little protection. Boetticher's account of the wild adventures of those eight years, *When, In Disgrace . . .*, inevitably expresses his sense of vindication and triumph in never compromising or quitting his task to return to Hollywood defeated. In this light it may be that Boetticher will want himself to be measured by the qualities of *Arruza* finally, rather than by those works whose stature and meaning depend on tradition, and to which I turn now.

The Ranown cycle: themes and world-view

Boetticher's westerns can be difficult to distinguish from each other given the recurrence of plots, locations, performers, even names. Therefore, it might be useful to begin by briefly summarizing the films:

Seven Men from Now (1956): Stride (Randolph Scott) tracks the seven men who held up the Wells Fargo station and killed his wife in Silver Springs. In the desert he meets and escorts an Eastern couple, the Greers, and is joined by two outlaws, Lee Marvin and Donald Barry, who are after the stolen gold which Greer is secretly transporting. After Indian attacks and the death of the killers, Stride guns down Marvin in a face-off.

The Tall T (1957): After losing his horse in a bet that he can ride a bull, Brennan (Randolph Scott) hitches a ride on a stage driven by an old friend, Rintoon, which carries the honeymooning Mimses and is mistakenly held up by Richard Boone, Henry Silva and Skip Homeier. Brennan and the woman, who is an heiress, are kept alive while word is sent to her father. Undermining the trust of the outlaws in one another, Brennan separates and kills them.

Decision at Sundown (1957): Bart Allison (Randolph Scott) and Sam (Noah Beery, Jnr) ride into the town where Tate Kimbrough (John Carroll), the man who had an affair with Allison's wife before she killed herself, is about to be married. Interrupting the ceremony with a promise to kill the groom, Allison takes cover in a stable with Sam. The brutal murder of the latter – in part the result of Allison's rejection of his friend's attempts to describe other infidelities of his wife's – affects the cowed citizenry who disarm the villain's henchmen, thus forcing a fair fight between Allison and Kimbrough which is cut short when Valerie French shoots her lover in the shoulder to save him.

Buchanan Rides Alone (1958): Riding into corrupt Agrytown, Buchanan (Randolph Scott) is arrested with Juan, a young Mexican of wealthy family who has killed Roy Agry for molesting his sister. While the Agrys try to cheat each other of ransom money, the hero's death is averted by one of the gang, Pecos, who commits himself to his fellow West Texan, Buchanan, the two then freeing Juan. However, Pecos is killed and the two recaptured, escaping finally to engage in a shoot-out where members of the Agry gang find themselves caught on a bridge in a crossfire. Carbo (Craig Stevens), Simon Agry's henchman, inherits the town as Buchanan rides off.

Ride Lonesome (1959): Brigade (Randolph Scott) arrests Billy John (James Best) and returns him to town slowly, since he is after Billy's brother Frank who long ago hanged Brigade's wife. The hero is joined by two outlaws, Pernell Roberts and James Coburn, who want Billy because an amnesty has been declared on any who bring him in, and by Mrs Lane (Karen Steele) whose husband has been killed by Indians. After the death of Frank, Brigade and Roberts face off, but the hero relents and leaves Billy and Mrs Lane to the outlaws who carry on without him.

Comanche Station (1960): Cody (Randolph Scott) buys Mrs Lowe (Nancy Gates) from the Comanche and in returning her to her husband who has offered a large reward is joined by Claude Akins, Skip Homeier and Richard Rust. Homeier is killed by Indians and Rust by Akins when he refuses to ambush the couple. Killing the villain, Cody then returns the woman to her husband, who is blind, and rides off into the mountains.

The perennial evocation of Hemingway does little to illuminate Boetticher's work; if we must look for literary parallels, Chaucer seems more appropriate. Above all, Boetticher's films are *comedies*, deeply ironic works, but comedies all the same. In contrast with the tragic world of Anthony Mann, Boetticher's small films are bitter-sweet reflections on the human condition. Within this perspective Chaplin and Lubitsch seem as relevant as Ford and Hawks for an understanding of Boetticher. Serious anatomies of the inadequacies of different attitudes to life, Boetticher's movies exist as *parodies* of the morality play, insisting on a sophisticated relationship with the audience, an agreement to reject simplistic notions of good and evil and to recognize that violence and injustice are less the property of malignant individuals than of the world itself. No one ever feels the impulse to hiss a Boetticher villain. Created with great care, these most human and sympathetic of men are always invariably blasted, to our sorrow. That these charming rogues must die is an index of how hostile and finally *absurd* the world is.

Typically, the hero is both a victim and a product, an expression, of this world; often we can feel that he functions as its *tool*. The variations in the hero, and his development, can be seen if we group the films so:

(a) *Seven Men from Now* and *Decision at Sundown*: In both of these the hero's wife has been killed relatively recently. In the first, characteristically, the hero has withdrawn into a coldness, tempered a trifle by guilt at having been indirectly responsible for his wife's death, which makes him somewhat inhuman. Lee Marvin's stylish lust for Annie Greer forces the hero to intervene, the growing involvement softening the character. In

Decision at Sundown an earlier, less mature version of the hero has become virtually unbalanced, a dark and tragic figure in Mann style. Here the action forces the hero to see that his revenge is meaningless, the character riding out bitter and alone, close to the ground later heroes already inhabit.

(*b*) *The Tall T* and *Buchanan Rides Alone*: In both of these the heroes are jaunty, philosophical men going about their business and suddenly surrounded by danger. The first, one of Boetticher's finest works, begins as a broad comedy and rapidly darkens with the deaths of Rinton, Hank and Jeff, his small boy, all of whom are thrown into a well. Here again the hero withdraws into a granite-like circumspection, only relieved by his relationship with Mrs Mims. In the second the hero remains jaunty and something of an irrelevance, the tone consistently comic (barring the death of Pecos).

(*c*) *Ride Lonesome* and *Comanche Station*: Here the roots of the action are long ago. 'I most forgot,' says Frank of his hanging of Brigade's wife. In the second film the abduction of Cody's wife by the Indians is ten years old; yet the character persists 'all the time alone, all the time in Comanche country'. In these works, the closest to the original structure of *Seven Men from Now*, the character is now absurd.

It was Bazin who first pointed out the resemblance of Randolph Scott to W. S. Hart: certainly Scott's archaic presence is a crucial factor in the films. An actor with an innate sense of his qualities and range, Scott had begun to restrict himself to western roles early in the forties. Like the Mann/Stewart films, the Ranown cycle gave a fillip to a declining career, the films intelligently structured round the star to ring the changes on a presence that could evoke anything from a cheerfully optimistic pragmatism to the unbending reticence of a beleaguered man in the twilight of his days.

In general, the Boetticher hero as created by Scott can be said to possess (or be moving towards) a great serenity, the knowledge that we are fundamentally alone, that nothing lasts, that what matters in the face of all this is 'living the way a man should'. Especially in the later films the hero has had it all – love, position, security – and lost it all. This makes the figure oddly anachronistic, a man who continues to assert values out of an image of himself that has its roots in the past. The essence of the hero is the knowledge that action is both gratuitous and essential. Revenge is meaningless

97

since the wife is dead; yet it is necessary because it is evidence of a way of life that the hero embodies: 'Some things a man can't ride around.' This stoicism arms the character with a grace that is an impenetrable armour against the temptations and threats of life. In this context, despite the ironic tone of the films, the absurd plight of a hero often menaced or held in bondage, there is finally a great dignity about the figure. The villain, for instance, always knows that there is no way of achieving his goal apart from 'going over' Scott: if the hero can be taken from behind, his code demands that he be confronted. The character has no magic; he is not the perfect shot or the fastest gun: only in *Seven Men from Now*, the loosest because the first of the series, does Scott have a mysterious expertise, felling Lee Marvin in the showdown like a dazed bull. More typically, the hero survives through intelligent calculation and a capacity for self-control in facing danger. Thus, at the outset of *Ride Lonesome* Brigade rides into Billy John's camp to find himself surrounded by a gang in the rocks. Turning the trap to his advantage, Brigade simply threatens to kill Billy on the spot, putting his own life on the line, unless the men are ordered away. The opening of *Comanche Station* is equally forceful, Cody moving through an arroyo, the crests of which are suddenly covered with Comanche. Instantly, the figure dismounts and unpacks trade goods, gracefully gesturing up to the Indians like a matador before his judges, his 'cool' unblown and intact.

This equilibrium, an essential expression of the hero's integrity, springs from his complete knowledge of the world through which he moves with the precision and skill of a dancer. The opening of Boetticher's original scenario of *Two Mules for Sister Sara* establishes a characteristic version of the hero:

It's rock country and the bleached-white spires burst jaggedly up through the desert sand in a wavering line opposite the setting sun, from south to north, where they grow in stature and seeming dignity to eventually jut their way into becoming a part of the Sierra Madre. As we scan the terrain we discover an almost imperceptible movement mostly hidden in the long evening shadows tight against the rocks. Zooming closer we recognize the figures as a lone rider astride his horse; followed by a pack-pony, loose, who trots to keep up with the long-legged animal

before him. The saddle horse is a blood red roan; a thoroughbred. . . .
The man is tall and lean, dressed in the colours of the desert and the
rocks. The tans, and the browns, and the grays of his tight-fitting outfit
are only broken up by the black and yellow beaded Indian moccasins
which he wears instead of boots. The plain leather holster of his Colt
revolver is thong-tied tight down just, above his right knee, and his long-
gun, a Winchester, swings slightly with the movement of his animal, in
a dirty canvas scabbard attached to the saddle just behind his left leg. A
new leather case containing U.S. binoculars hangs from the saddle's
pommel. And now we get our first real close look at the man himself. It
is impossible to determine his age. He could be thirty, or maybe even
forty, but we'll never be sure because the wrinkles around his eyes and
at the corner of his tight lips could have come into being from the desert
sun. He wears his sweat-stained hat low down over his eyes to shade them
from the fading light, but there is a sparkle of all-consuming awareness
in those eyes that makes you feel certain that not even a lizard mor'n half
a mile away could skitter across the sand without his knowing which way
it was headed. Unpleasantly there is an aura of meanness about the man.
Watching him you smell the sticky odour of hate that seemingly envelops
everything around him except his horse. But in spite of the meanness that
you feel, or the suspicion that his deep-rooted loathing includes even the
sand and the rocks, you are suddenly overwhelmingly aware that the man
is all-over, downright, beautiful. Even the slight movement of his body
as he swings his head and shoulders around to check his pack-pony is
cat-like and deadly. . . .

A somewhat darker figure than usual, the hero here is typical in
other respects. Riding easily through the world to which he belongs,
the character carries everything that he needs with him. He is
invulnerable so long as he is alone: once he meets with others he
will insist on travelling in the open, aware that he is now exposed.
Although danger lurks everywhere, it is most common where the
desert offers the illusion of safety or life: at a deserted swing
station, a green oasis, atop a ridge or in a cave. The terrain is
barren and hostile, a cruel and empty landscape, permanent and
unchanging, that dwarfs the figures who move through it for a
time. 'A man needs a reason to ride this country. You got a reason?'
Suspicious of all he meets, the hero himself needs no reason: the
desert is his domain. While others sleep the hero sits erect and
alone, ever on guard.

In both *Seven Men from Now* and *The Tall T* the hero admits

The development of the hero (reading across): *Seven Men from Now, Decision
at Sundown, The Tall T, Buchanan Rides Alone, Ride Lonesome, Comanche
Station* →

that he is afraid, and he and the heroine are allowed to touch, the audience offered the possibility that at the end they have come together. If the heroes of *Decision at Sundown* and *Buchanan Rides Alone* are both fearless in their different ways, they are not allowed to kill their antagonist (Kimbrough, Carbo), and thus are softened despite the absence of women. However, in *Ride Lonesome* and *Comanche Station* we cannot believe that the hero experiences the emotions that we do. Here nothing is possible between the hero and heroine, the decorum unbroken, the distance unbridgeable. In these works – especially the second where he destroys the villain – the hero has ceased to be a man altogether. In his purest expression the core of the Boetticher hero is apparent, the figure existing as a *spirit* rather than a person, a *way* of life rather than a life. An abstraction, the hero represents an unrealizable ideal, an experience and knowledge of the world so complete that the character is finally as impervious as the rocks around him. But if it were possible to become like Boetticher's Scott, we would hesitate. A man beyond all human ties, the character is *impotent*, never initiating action, ever passively responding. There is no drama in the figure, for this has been played out in the past (*Decision at Sundown*): every encounter now is simply the occasion for a ritualistic reaffirmation of a choice forced upon the hero long ago.

This absurdity in the character's position is the source of the duality which Boetticher exploits in the films. At times the hero is the very butt of the world, tossed about like a leaf, tragi-comically at the mercy of life. At others the character *is* the world itself, as relentless as the landscape, as regular and predictable as the seasons. This interplay accounts for the comic range of Boetticher's work which extends from the farce of *Buchanan Rides Alone*, where the hero is bewilderingly shuttled in and out of menacing situations repeatedly, to the bitter irony of *Decision at Sundown* or *The Tall T*. However, regardless of the mode of the film, the hero himself remains a source of amusement. For in order to survive the character has had to adopt a colourless and severe style, the main feature of which is a laconic frankness. Where others, like Mr Mims, shoot off their mouths, and where the villain, Richard

Boone, for example, often *needs* talk, the hero knows that language can be dangerous: 'A man can talk himself to death.' Villains are ever confessing to Scott that when 'a man gets half-way, he oughta have something of his own, something to belong to, be proud of'; the hero always replies stolidly: 'They say that.' Where the villain comments in detail on the desirability of the woman, Scott agrees: 'She ain't ugly.' Using in a very disciplined way the cracker-barrel tradition of humorous observation that runs through the western, Boetticher creates the hero as a plain dealer, a sophisticated yet rural figure, a Will Rogers with six-guns. In the same vein is the character's quaint courtliness, even when angry dismissing the heroine with a sharp compliment: 'You cook good coffee. Good *night*, Mrs Lowe.' A source of great humour, these qualities also contribute to our sense of the fabulous in the character, evoking a code by which he lives despite his circumstances. This is even clearer in the blunt, gritty aphorisms that are infrequently wrung from him: 'A man oughta be able to look after his woman.'

If half of the Boetticher hero is a sad clown, the other half is a *kill-joy*. For the basic deception in the films of the Ranown cycle, the key to their dramatic structure, is that the Randolph Scott figure is the hero only in a technical sense: it is, of course, the villain who is our true hero. Boetticher's villains are so important that one can claim the stronger they are, the stronger the film, tracing a slowly descending curve from *The Tall T*'s Richard Boone through the three journey films (Roberts and Coburn, Akins and Rust, Marvin) to *Decision at Sundown*, which only really comes alive when John Carroll has to muster the courage to face what he feels will be certain death, and *Buchanan Rides Alone*, where Craig Stevens's Carbo is as amusing and marginal as the hero himself. Here Boetticher forsakes characters of integrity to play with the Agry family whom he creates as *humours* in the medieval sense, farcical expressions of ignorance and greed. Even the weak *Westbound*, a bad script which Boetticher shot reluctantly for Warners in 1959 so that he could make *The Rise and Fall of Legs Diamond* the following year, is enlivened by its heavies, Andrew Duggan and Michael Pate.

Typically, Boetticher's villains differ from the Scott figure in their comparatively flamboyant style, ever sporting a shocking touch of green or pink, a colourful Indian armlet, a fancy draw. Within the community, this impulse can produce a villain that has the splendour of a peacock, the immaculately tailored Carbo amongst all the sweaty Agrys, Kimbrough in his white shirt complete with ruffles. Where the hero is ever ready to 'say out in words' exactly what he means, the villain is as likely to tell us a story which soon begins to sound very like the situation that the characters are in: 'Once knew a gal looked just like you, Mrs Greer.' Cocksure of himself, Marvin tells his tale with great charm, virtually ravishing Annie verbally in the process, and wholly disrupts the ritual of shared coffee while the hero sits helpless. It is this narcissim, the need to entertain and *dazzle*, that often does the villain in. Above all, the character must dominate, imposing himself and taking on the world single-handedly. Thus Marvin and Akins both shoot down their minions ruthlessly; Boone is cheerful on finding Silva and Homeier, the 'animals' as he calls them, both dead.

Yet Boetticher insists that the villain shares a certain integrity with the hero. This is evident in a strict rule of the drama whereby the Scott figure is saved by a gratuitous act of the villain's: thus Lee Marvin guns down one of the killers about to shoot Stride in the back; Boone keeps Brennan out of the well; Pernell Roberts bluffs Billy into dropping the carbine he holds to Brigade's middle; Akins rides into an Indian attack to help Cody. 'It seemed like a good idea.' The villain knows that his act will not matter when the final confrontation comes; yet his idea of himself compels a rescue of the man who may (and usually does) destroy him. Some Boetticher villains are darker than others: where Marvin and Akins seem driven by self-aggrandisement – to be the top gun, the head man, 'number one' – both Boone and Roberts are trying to retire from outlawry, to find 'a place' and escape being 'all the time alone'. The great power of these works follows from poising the major villain in the existential moment that is essential to Boetticher; in both *Seven Men from Now* and *Comanche Station* the locating of this drive to 'cross over' within essentially innocent characters (both Greer and Dobie turn their backs on evil and are promptly riddled with bullets) results in a drama of less force.

This action, together with the structure of Boetticher's films, may suggest that this vision is a moral one, the films 'floating poker-games', as Andrew Sarris once called them, in which each character must decide how to live. But, fundamentally, the action of the films is a dialogue between villain and hero which masks the attempt of the villain to *become* the hero, a reaching out for power or experience that the hero embodies. Whether a dark figure or not, Boetticher's villain remains a deeply attractive figure for us – we understand him in a way we cannot the hero – and the films stand finally as celebrations of this character who attempts to *create* action in a way that the static Scott cannot. 'I couldn't have enjoyed the five thousand if I'd done you that way.' Bitterly ironic it is that the thrust and style of the villain make him vulnerable by exposing him to the very ideal he aspires to. At the end of both *The Tall T* and *Comanche Station* the villain stands with his back to Scott, safe for the moment; in the earlier work, the point is explicit, Richard Boone walking carefully to his horse and then riding out alive. But finally in both cases the character – a man of great life and wit who has given us much pleasure – turns to confront the world and an absurd, relentlessly dour justice which utterly destroys him.

At points Boetticher insists that the villain can survive if he resists the pull of narcissism to embrace meaningful relationships. This is of course implied by the hero who, while resolutely alone, carries the scars of past involvements. Tate Kimbrough, a figure who clearly looks forward to Legs Diamond, is only saved by Lucy's act of love, shooting him as he faces Scott and thus forcing him to accept his need for her. Carbo, who is allowed to emerge as the head man of Agrytown at the end, perhaps deserves this for his steadfast loyalty to Simon Agry in an atmosphere rife with intrigue and betrayal. Certainly Pernell Roberts, the one character to survive to a life of amnesty with Karen Steele, alone of major villains enjoys a relationship of real warmth with another character, James Coburn's Wid. However, given the dialectic of the hero and the

The Boetticher villain: style and narcissism: *Seven Men from Now, Decision at Sundown*

Comanche Station; The Rise and Fall of Legs Diamond

thrust of the villain, it is not surprising that Boetticher's view of social relationships is ambiguous. Marriages are pathetic, shattered by death, betrayed, or weak; the optimism of even *Ride Lonesome* diminishes if we consider that Roberts may be on the threshold of the cycle through which Scott has passed. In *The Tall T* Mrs Mims has married a cowardly carpet-bagger to escape her loneliness; in both *Comanche Station* and *Westbound* the husbands are cripples, dependent on their women. As with Anthony Mann, characters often muse on a pastoral future, 'a place' just north of the Sonora, just west of the Pecos. Yet the typical community within the films is that of the camp-fire, the only ritual that of the meal, people passing the coffee-pot. Groups never exist in Boetticher, the action almost always developed through a series of dialogues. Sitting on guard in the shadows, the hero is visited first by the heroine and then by the villain; the minor villains talk, perhaps interrupted by their leader who then passes on to the woman.

A similar ambiguity cloaks the heroine. The scripts insist that the woman is important because she assuages loneliness and offers meaningful contact – she is the keeper of 'the place'. However, this spiritual view is undercut as the films unwind, the heroine invariably taking on overtones of great physical desirability. Boetticher's women always suffer indignities, forced to stand in a downpour, tripping into mud, ducked in a water-trough; yet they come out sparkling, their often tattered clothes hugging their bodies. Even Maureen O'Sullivan's homely and ageing Mrs Mims takes on sexual qualities sharpened for us when, humiliated, she bares herself to tempt Skip Homeier to his death. However, it is Karen Steele who is Boetticher's definitive heroine, at once a good-natured warm companion and a hard sexual object.

Inevitably, Boetticher's individualism naturally moves towards its close neighbour, the Hawksian ethic, and a separating out of the men from the boys or, in Boetticher's terms, the *aficionados* from the crowd. If weaker characters in Hawks aren't 'good enough', in Boetticher we could say that men who 'run on the gentle side' lack *cojones*. Thus, although the films insist on a dignity for hero and villains, this does not extend to a Willard Mims, whose name

The heroine: Karen Steele in *Westbound*

sums him up. Similarly, if Boetticher's women do not have to become men to be taken seriously (as Hawks's must), they remain somewhat on the margins, their shifting *persona* reflecting the drives of hero and villain. Living within the desert, speaking true, functioning man to man, these imply accepting a love that can finally be crippling. Trying to top the world, to sparkle, to be *the* man, this can mean using the woman mechanically, the individual attempting in vain to remain invulnerable.

The Ranown Cycle: Form and Style

The moral of Boetticher's films is thus a simple one: everyone loses. Life defeats charm, innocence is blasted. The world is finally a sad and funny place, life a tough, amusing game which can never be won but must be played. If Boetticher's films can darken to near-tragedy, the pessimism is always held in check by an innate response to the absurdity of it all, the way in which we are forced

Buchanan Rides Alone: threats of death

to take up roles in a *farce*. It is this comic awareness in Boetticher that is behind what appears a natural classicism, a fascination with formal aspects of the drama and the terrain on which it is played out.

Boetticher clearly takes a sympathetic delight in the way in which his characters always find themselves under the gun, often trapped in the middle of a circle of stress. In the journey films, which almost invariably culminate in the setting of an *arena*, this action is constant. The group is at once under the threat of a hostile environment (Indians are all round them) and functions as a source of menace internally for the hero, the dramatic action a mirror-image of the world the character inhabits. Often the action itself seems circular or *cyclical*, the hero advancing not at all on ground he commands at the outset. The foundation for the very production of the Ranown films, this key movement structures many of Boetticher's earlier works as well. Hence *The Cimarron Kid*, Boetticher's first western, opens with the hero's release from prison and ends with his arrest; *Seminole* begins and closes with the Indians resolutely independent of the white man; *The Man from the Alamo* opens with the departure of the hero from the fight against Santa Anna and ends with his return. In both *Decision at Sundown* and *Buchanan Rides Alone* Boetticher plays with this movement within the plot very self-consciously, in the first Allison being visited in his besieged stable by a parade of interested parties, in the second the Agrys, their henchmen, and Buchanan, all changing places as they conspire to achieve their ends.

This impulse at a formal level accounts for the great elegance and grace of Boetticher's work. Typically, *Seven Men from Now* opens *in medias res*, Scott creeping through the desert to come on two of his wife's killers sheltering in a cave on a stormy night. In the morning Scott moves out through the sun-bleached terrain to crest a rise and discover the Greers, their wagon mired in the mud. After a scene of great delicacy, the men washing the carthorses in a limpid pool as Annie bathes round the bend, the oasis is left behind, the party moving on deeper into the desert. After its light-hearted opening *The Tall T*, although not a journey film, takes on

Comanche Station (opposite and above): formal consistency

a similar movement. In both *Ride Lonesome* and *Comanche Station* the construction and pace are tightly controlled, the action unwinding with spell-binding formal rigour, the films finally resembling pure ritual. Seizing on the cyclical pattern of the journey western, the alternation of drama and lyricism, tension and release, intimacy and space, Boetticher gradually refines it to arrive at the remarkable balance of an ambiguous world poised between tragedy and pastoral comedy.

The meaning in a Boetticher movie resides less in its bright moments of good humour, its dark moments of violence, than in the continuum, a seasonal movement, a perpetual interplay of light and shade, success and decline, life and death. Spiralling through day and following night, the drama remains ever in the foreground, the settings changing religiously as different stages are reached on the journey, yet somehow not changing at all, the desert finally the dominant place. Thus *Ride Lonesome* moves through three days and nights, the company pushing on over dangerous open vistas of arid country each morning and afternoon to cluster in the dappled dark of an evening camp. If dusk is often a kind, contemplative time for talk of the future, danger rides in bright and early at sun-up to temper hope and throttle dreams. There is one moment in particular here that with great economy and resonance seems to express the heart of Boetticher's world. As the party move out from the swing station after the visit of Indians who hope to barter the dead husband's horse for the wife, the camera follows them from inside the building. The dark outlines of the roof and porch frame the image, the eye drawn out past the silhouetted horse-rail to the bright clearing, the rocky hills and misty mountains beyond. In the left-hand corner of the scope frame a water-vase hangs from the porch roof, gently swaying. Four times the eye is drawn across the frame as the group ride out in single file, each character moving into vision from the right and trotting across out of sight to the left, the camera panning with the last rider to frame the whole group as they move into the desert. This briefest of images has a narrative function – the shot is repeated when Frank and his gang approach the station – but the composition and lighting are so delicate that they finally are a pleasure in themselves. The tension between static black border and bright rhythmic play within is so fine that ultimately the image has the quality, the essence of Boetticher, of an animated still-life.

At moments like these Boetticher achieves a formal rigour and philosophical nuance that recall the most unlikely of parallels, the Japanese master Yasujiro Ozu. Certainly a common factor is the evocation of a sadly ephemeral life in a world, beautiful in itself, which remains apart and unchanging. Landscape in Boetticher always has a conceptual weight, signifying a lonely and hostile universe. Often this relentless primeval world is bordered by a lush, green Arcadia: both *Seven Men from Now* and *The Tall T* move from a pastoral setting into the desert; *Ride Lonesome* and *Comanche Station* reverse the pattern. However, always in Boetticher there is a formal interest in landscape, an observation and delight that give the images a *decorative* value. Often what we have is very like a painting, the characters moving over brutal terrain in the foreground, the middle distance a wall of jagged spires, the great peaks of the Sierras in the misty background beyond. As Bazin was quick to point out with reference to *Seven Men from Now*, the very texture of the rocks, like the faces of horses, give Boetticher a pleasure which he communicates directly to his audience.

This aesthetic delight in pattern, colour and movement – simply, in creating beautiful images – is paralleled by Boetticher's joy in *playing* with the recurrent elements of his form. If these films strike us as highly *civilized* works, it is because of the studied awareness with which certain rites are enacted. Nowhere is this more in evidence than in the fact of Boetticher's having worked to a formula: of course *Seven Men from Now*, *The Tall T*, *Ride Lonesome* and *Comanche Station* are essentially the same film. Moreover, both *Decision at Sundown* and *Buchanan Rides Alone*, which have structural similarities, can be seen as loose transpositions of *The Tall T* into the setting of the community. The word 'formula' is important and must be insisted on: often it is the heaviest club in a critic's armoury, reserved for the mechanical and repetitive. Yet Boetticher's movies are both personal and refreshing precisely because of their given structure which frees him to achieve his distinctive ironic and comic effects.

Any view of Hollywood, any theory of mass culture, that excludes a Boetticher must be a sadly impoverished one. But it would be euphemistic to describe this level of popular art as unpretentious. In a genre only the epic tip of which has drawn any consistent attentions, Boetticher's small films are very nearly the bottom of the iceberg: co-feature-length formula exercises built round a minor star in the tradition of Tom Mix, Roy Rogers and Hopalong Cassidy. Yet Boetticher's care is admirable, the direction never inflating into solemnity nor lapsing into slackness, but meeting the material head-on with obvious affection. Burt Kennedy's tendency as a script-writer to repeat (and steal from) himself in playing on time-honoured patterns of the western could not have found a better home. Responding with sympathy and wit to ritualistic elements, Boetticher achieves a range of cosmic expression that provides the basic tone of his pictures.

(*a*) verbal play: repetition, variation and surprise are of course fundamental to comedy, and a feature of Boetticher's own scripts as well as those with Kennedy. 'Buchanan's the name,' announces the hero cockily everywhere he goes in Agrytown, clearly asking for the trouble he gets. 'Do you want to hear the rest of the story?' Lee Marvin endlessly asks as he sits grinning over his coffee at the Greers and the silent Scott. 'I'd hate to have to kill you' – 'I'd hate to have you try': some such formulaic exchange often passes between hero and villain. Similarly, a rhetorical question is always amusingly undercut: 'Do you think I love him any the less?' – 'Yes, Mam.'

(*b*) play with settings and props: the pleasure Boetticher derives from landscape often results in a sharp contrast of tight places – caves and crevices – and vast open country, the scope frame filled with desert on which small dots move. On many occasions we can feel that these settings function as a *stage*. Characters are always passing each other either cups of coffee or guns, a measure of how abstracted the action is from social norms, but also a source of paradox and irony (as well as movement within the frame). Villains throw the hero a gun, but show little respect for the ritual of the meal. In *Buchanan Rides Alone* both Juan and the ransom for him function somewhat like props which the villains can never bring together. Juan's dancing horse (one of Boetticher's own, trained in *rejoneo*) also weaves in and out of the action.

(c) play with character: Boetticher often achieves a broad comedy while establishing his characters which, given the violence that follows, colours the action with a sad irony. The clearest example of this is *The Tall T*, where the opening rapidly introduces us to a whole range of juvenile genre elements: a jaunty hero thrown from a bull, a venerable Gabby Hayes of a mule-skinner in Arthur Hunnicutt's Rintoon, an admiring lad who asks the hero to buy him some striped candy, his lonely, talkative father who runs the swing station. Created with great warmth, the characters are rapidly destroyed, save for the hero who has to face the real bull of his world in the form of Henry Silva. Minor villains in Boetticher are always affectionately treated and are a source of both gentle humour (often they don't know their age but are 'mostly young') and great jokes. Hence in *Comanche Station* Rust and Homeier agree that although it may be desirable to 'amount to something', the price of actually *working* would be too high. Homeier, insisting that all it would get a cowboy would be a decent burial, is left floating in a river moments later. James Coburn in *Ride Lonesome* is surprised that his partner of five years standing actually *likes* him: 'I never knew that.'

(d) play with situations: I have already referred to the disciplined way in which Boetticher structures action round dialogues which break the journey; also to his play with the situations of confinement and release, a delightful example of which occurs in *Ride Lonesome* where James Best holds a carbine to Scott's stomach, unsure of whether it is loaded, while Roberts trains a gun on *him*. *Decision at Sundown* opens with a sight gag, Scott a bearded tough who orders the stage he is aboard to stop at gunpoint, only to get off rather than rob it. Confrontations are always inflected in an original fashion by Boetticher. Hence the murder of Clete by Marvin, who then lights his cigarette from the one still smouldering in his side-kick's mouth, a comic act that none the less darkens the character for us and prepares us for his shocked death at Scott's hands. More typically, endings in Boetticher partake of a delicate irony, Boone in *The Tall T* escaping but forced to turn back by his respect for both Scott and himself, Frank in *Ride Lonesome* facing the hero's exquisite revenge – Billy strung up to the same tree from which the wife was hanged. Gravedigging scenes are always light-years away from John Ford, the only 'words' a few jokes from the villains as they dig away in a scruffy corner of the desert.

Predictably, Boetticher's humour can be cruel where weakness or cowardice are involved. Thus, although we hear a lecture in *Decision at Sundown* on how none of us can face ourselves as we really are, this doesn't alter the pleasure we get from the breaking of the whisky-bottle hidden in Zorin's pocket, the smug preacher

Confrontations: *Ride Lonesome* and *A Time for Dying*

exposed as a drinker. In the same way we relish (or seem to be asked to) the way in which both Andrew Duggan and John Carroll are forced to face the righteous figure of Scott without their supporting henchmen. Certainly the death of Willard Mims in *The Tall T* is surprisingly *funny*, Boone gently reassuring the character, then brutally giving the order ('Bust him, Chink') and showing genuine surprise at the suddenly widowed woman's grief. Similarly, the impulse to play with the audience in Boetticher can sometimes slip over the line into a manipulating or conning of the viewer. Thus, if the crippled Mr Lowe at the end of *Comanche Station* is dramatically right, given his introduction after the death of Akins, he is nevertheless something of a clever trick in answer to the questions the film itself sets about the husband. The irony of a prostitute dressed as a nun, the mask in place until the very end, also seems an unnecessary gimmick.

But characteristically Boetticher plays the game according to the rules, his respect for both audience and form evident in the way in which he disciplines his own experience in the service of the material. Thus, although there are echoes of the bullfight in Scott's attempt to ride and win a seed-bull in *The Tall T*, the scene owes less to the tradition of the *corrida* than to that of the rodeo, evoked at the outset where cowboys struggle with a bronc that bursts through the corral, dragging our hero behind it. Given Boetticher's preoccupation with bullfighting, one might have expected him to deepen the picture's tone, making the encounter more expressive of his themes. However, to have done so would have been to violate the drama, which here requires the hero be established as amusingly philosophical in the face of set-backs. The imagery of bullfighting often colours Boetticher's films, invariably coming into play where its rituals meaningfully coincide with those of the western. In *Comanche Station* Indians ride in on the hero with spears at the ready like *banderillas*. At the end of *Ride Lonesome* Frank charges Scott who stands like a matador ready for the kill. The carcass of Chink, like that of a dead bull, is dragged out of sight by a horse; moments later Boone's final charge ends with hands clutched to head as he wheels blindly, tearing a rough curtain from the mouth of a cave. Everywhere in Boetticher men turn their back on a gun – the majority to their peril. However, such moments, evidence of the personal nature of Boetticher's art, do not depend for their effect upon our awareness of the underlying metaphor, the action growing out naturally from the narrative which he treats with the utmost respect.

It is in the interaction of Boetticher's commitment to character and drama and his distinctively geometrical style that we have the final expression of the game. If often we feel that what we watch is a play within a play, it is not only because Boetticher's art, like sport, rests on inventive variations within the narrowest given limits. Nor is it wholly due to the way in which the films (recalling the action of Shakespeare's dark comedies) trace near-tragic patterns within a comic structure. Above all, the quality flows from the great tension of character and behaviour realized with a vivid particularity within a formal discipline that moves towards abstraction. Boetticher's gifts as a film-maker – intelligent dramatic organization and a creative use of actors, a fine sense of composition and pace – typically create a world that is both close and distant, action that is open and yet predetermined.

Always Boetticher uses the actual life-style of his performers (rewriting his scripts once the cast is set) to achieve a vigorous life within the drama. Developing with an elegant mathematical precision, the action pyramids, growing peaks of tautness alternating with a leisurely lyricism. The camera moves fluidly within the group as it makes its rounds, pausing here and there to record the play of issues, the counterpoint of character, within a static frame. As the figures move through landscape Boetticher stands back to fix them in the depth and perspective of eternity. Often as it dollies with the characters, the camera gradually brings into focus the black blur of danger on the horizon. Men are free to move: the world is hostile.

If finally nothing is possible but the game, we must be grateful that with these films Boetticher found a playing-field and ground rules when he most needed them. The strange accident of the Ranown cycle at last allowed the experience of fifteen years of professional attack and frustrated authority to find direction and purpose. Working consistently within a shared traditional form, ideal for the expression of his private world of a questing individualism, Boetticher slowly arrived at a *personal* tradition in the small glittering morality plays that emerged. At his best he achieved here a remarkable formal and dramatic control, *The Tall T*, *Ride Lonesome* and *Comanche Station* recalling the delicate perfection of finely cut gems, immaculately drawn miniatures. Working at virtually debased levels within the industry, Boetticher none the less found the ritual, at once personally sustaining and publicly meaningful, that he required.

Departure and Return

For Boetticher action exists only at the level of the individual: hence the absurd dilemma of existence, each man both a bullfighter and a bull. Strikingly, the villains of the Ranown cycle ride on the scene like matadors, flanked by their *banderilleros*, the darker ones committed to any encounter that will prove them 'el numero uno'. However, for the hero, whose scars, intelligence and poise are evidence of that status, these men are sleek brave bulls, narcissistic animals who charge into the arena completely unaware that others exist, shocked to discover their own vulnerability.

This internal dialectic is expressed in a very pure form in *The Rise and Fall of Legs Diamond*, made immediately after the Ranown cycle and a rare example of Boetticher being given considerable freedom (so long as the film kept its distance from the facts) in a different genre. Consequently, the opening promise of the film ('This is the way it happened'), although supported by sleazy twenties jazz, journalistic titles and a resolutely period look, is soon betrayed by Boetticher. Any idea of exposé is left far behind as the film moves forward wittily and gracefully, like its dancing hero, Legs Diamond's great quality, his strength and weakness, is his complete egotism, and we watch in fascination as he dazzles all with his footwork, exploiting his style and charm to get higher and higher up the ladder. Beginning with Karen Steele's humble, naïve Alice whose emotions he plays on brazenly ('I'm lonely'), Legs

cons a host of characters in order to get close to Arnold Rothstein, the king of gangsterdom. Both 'A.R.' and his mistress, Monica, fall for Legs's patter ('I'm a young man trying to get ahead') and are quickly discarded, Diamond soon reigning supreme from his base at the Hotsy Totsy Club where his first appearance had been as a dancer. At this point Legs seeks to free himself of ties that make him vulnerable, dooming his consumptive brother by refusing to pay medical bills. The moment is crucial: when he and Alice return from their comical tour of Europe's cinemas, Legs finds himself alone and facing the Syndicate. Turning to Monica in his desperation, Legs is betrayed to hoodlums one of whom masters his fear sufficiently for the kill.

The great flaw in this impressive work is its jarring shift of tone from elegant comedy, which is the film's basic mode and is admirably sustained from the outset, into the dark, tragic vein of its last few minutes. That the film flies apart here is due wholly to the traditions of the gangster picture which are not amenable to Boetticher's philosophical preoccupations. Within these conventions, Legs's fall is partly historical, his old-style individualism overtaken by the corporate capitalism of the underworld boardroom. To some extent Diamond's need to confront individuals man to man, to dominate through the personal encounter and to avoid all forms of organization, makes this resolution meaningful. However, the drive of the script and action is at a deeper level: 'As long as one person in the world loved you, you were safe . . . that was the magic.' Like a narcissistic matador or a stereotype of the movie star, Legs feeds off the image that he projects and that is reflected back by those he exploits. Movies bore Legs because he lives one, his life one long game which he plays brilliantly, adopting whatever *persona* – small-town lad, sycophant, hero, lover – the situation requires. In this light the tragedy of Legs is that, like the entertainer, he realizes too late that without an audience he has no role. Thinking that the game can be won – that he can achieve immortality – Legs loses by eliminating all the other players.

This philosophical thematic, while clarifying the action of the film, does not excuse its broken quality or the moral rhetoric of

123

The Rise and Fall of Legs Diamond: Ray Danton as Legs

The Rise and Fall of Legs Diamond: Legs (Ray Danton) and Alice (Karen Steele)

the end (Legs is the one Boetticher character to get an epitaph: 'He never loved anybody . . . that's why he's dead'). The decline of Legs is altogether too arbitrary and mechanical, the ravished innocence of Alice, while delicately expressed in the film, finally an insubstantial judgement on this charming Boetticher rogue. Thus the central confusion in the picture is between the Classical structure, which demands a tragic, precipitate fall, and Boetticher's attempts to satisfy it by having an invulnerable villain, who *is* the hero here, defeat *himself*. Not surprisingly, the result is that *The Rise and Fall of Legs Diamond* is mostly *rise*.

It would be tempting to see this elegant film as Boetticher's bitter farewell, the action in these terms a private parable about success and failure in the smart Hollywood jungle. But in going to Mexico Boetticher was not renouncing his past; nor did he know he was leaving for eight years rather than eight months. Simply, *Arruza* became both a test and a debt, a proof of himself and an obligation both to his original idea and the famous matador. Not surprisingly, therefore, the long-awaited *Arruza* is an important work in every respect: a deeply personal film, a valuable record, a moving experience. It is Boetticher's labour of love, a personal tribute, and the outcome of fifteen years of planning and effort.

In tracing how Arruza comes out of retirement on two occasions – first as a *rejoneador*, later to fight in Plaza Mexico – Boetticher celebrates one of the greatest performers in the ritual that has been so important in his own life. The action in the arena is treated with great care, the point of view changing fluidly to follow the beauty of the rider and his horse circling endlessly before the bull, the *corridas* themselves, models of grace and courage, quietly observed by the respectful camera. Boetticher's sense of humour gives the film a characteristic warmth, the commentary guying Arruza for thinking the most expensive horse must be the best (the mount, like a Boetticher hero, turns out to be wary of circular enclosures), the film recording the amusing tests administered to the cows, playing with the faces of jealous matadors, disgruntled at Arruza's skill. Dominating the picture, Arruza is evoked in simple, idealized terms, his family sketched in the background. The style and movement of the picture, despite its documentary nature and the narration, recall the westerns, the action shifting regularly from quiet, lyrical moments at Pasteje, Arruza's bull-breeding ranch, to the high drama of the arena. The farewell appearance is exemplary, the audacity of the *rejoneo* giving way to an extraordinary series of passes, the man a graceful statue as the bull charges past repeatedly, culminating with Arruza astonishingly killing the bull according to Boetticher's plan for the camera. The film opens with an elegant series of zooms in on matadors of the past enshrined in statuary surrounding the plaza, a motif returned to when Arruza visits the empty ring before deciding to return a second time. This imagery is extended by the freezing of the final frame – Arruza radiant as he circles the ring with his trophies on high – after we have heard that the matador died, meaninglessly, in a car crash some months later. But, the narrator insists, no man is dead while he is still remembered.

In 1951 with *The Bullfighter and the Lady* Boetticher had seized on a sure dramatic structure in using his own experience, the film tracing the growth to maturity of a young American learning to fight bulls. The action of *The Magnificent Matador* was less successful, a melodrama describing a top matador's flight from the ring to escape introducing his illegitimate son to the bulls. The tautness of the opening here was eventually betrayed in a relaxed scene where Anthony Quinn tries to tell the boy laconically sipping soup that he is his father: 'Yes, I know, Matador.' Moving through what seem to be obligatory scenes for Hollywood bullfighting films – the matador pursued by an American woman, the drawing of the bulls, scenes of prayer before the *corrida* – the film comes alive only in the tour of Pasteje, a sequence of extreme long-shots on the black dots moving over a range drenched with sharp, pure sunlight, culminating in Quinn's fight with a bull against the timeless setting of mountains and sky.

If *Arruza* in many respects transcends Hollywood treatment of the subject, if the film must stand as a fine work its power is nevertheless diminished (as in the latter picture) by the nature of its fundamentally static hero. For while capturing for us the most dramatic moments of isolated action, *Arruza*'s own dramatic action is *motion*. Like the Scott hero, Carlos Arruza is complete and serene when we meet him, the film only recording countless confirmations of who he is. Inevitably, the single most important and dramatic moment in Arruza's life – his absurd death – occurs off-stage and is denied by the film.

In twenty-five years as a film-maker, Boetticher has made many small movies only a dozen or so of which have been westerns. However, in the eyes of both the industry and criticism, he has existed only within this genre. Now, *Arruza* at last completed, Boetticher seems prepared to accept and work within this role, his return to Hollywood marked (self-consciously as always) with a small western shot on the eighteen-day schedule typical of the earlier pictures. Moreover, the film emerges from a production context that in many ways recalls the Ranown cycle, the company of actors and stuntmen a small one of old veterans except for two or three featured newcomers, the photographer a favourite of Boetticher's, Lucien Ballard, the producer a friend, Audie Murphy.

His in every detail from original script to final cut, *A Time for Dying* is even more studied in its play of formal and dramatic elements than many of the earlier works. Thus the film describes a perfect circle for all of its principals: the aspiring gunfighter, Cass, dying outside the brothel from which he saves Nellie at the outset; Nellie herself returned, again alone, to the setting she fled; Billy Pimple with his outriders drifting back into the rocks and trees from which they appeared to confront Cass in the beginning. As well the film has both an overture – Cass's rescue of a rabbit from a rattler ('Run, little feller, run for your life') ironically establishing the film's theme of unprotected innocence – and a coda, the final images of a second young Nellie making for Mamie's, which announces the beginning of another cycle.

Although the landscape here is Arizona ridge and cactus rather than California's Lone Pine rock formations, the interplay of barren open range and pastoral forest faithfully evokes Boetticher's world of the morality play. His two pilgrims are mocked by the cycles of freedom and confinement, hope and humiliation, through which they move. Ironically, the couple suffer and Cass dies, not because of his disruptive heroism (saving Nellie, foiling the bank robbery), but for his foolish bravado and exhibitionism: his killing of the rattler and his sharpshooting in the saloon leading to the encounters with Billy, his fancy gunplay for Nellie attracting Jesse James and his boys. Although James warns the couple clear of Silver City, Cass stubbornly rides on, to meet more of James's men who surround them and steal Nellie to dress up their party in the attempt on the bank.

Having stopped the hold-up, Cass hears applause for the last time. He is called out into the street by Pimple (or William C. *Cootes*, as he insists), a second-rate matador in comparison with the stylish 'el numero uno' of Audie Murphy's James. Original as ever – the two men are comically caught with guns at their back – the final confrontation is made explicitly theatrical as well, Cass and Billy standing in spotlights on the empty stage, their faces

A Time for Dying: Victor Jory as Judge Roy Bean

half-masks of light and darkness. The comedy ('Billy, that girl pull a hammer down on you, I'll blow her husband's head clear across the street.' – 'Ben, this girl pull a hammer down on me, it don't do no good what you do with her husband's head') recedes, the play growing dark with the snake's revenge on the rabbit, the innocent *novillero* making the final discovery of what life is about in his meaningless death.

'One of those fellas always loses.' An inane circle of violence, an absurd but compulsory play of comic suffering, Vinegaroon's game of rock, scissors and paper describes the action of the film and the core of Boetticher's ironic vision. Vinegaroon itself, less a town than an extension and a summary of the world through which the couple move, is presided over by the spectacle of Victor Jory's Judge Roy Bean. The ruler of the game – this funny, monstrous old man, this evil clown – is a brilliant expression by Boetticher of life's absurdity. A humour in the tradition of the Agrys, the character of Bean at once evokes drunkenness and sloth, greed and self-love; but above all he is *variability* itself. Sternly lecturing youth on its presumption one moment, nostalgically reminiscing on a Lily Langtry he has never met the next, brutally hanging one apple-cheeked lad, benevolently forcing a marriage on Cass and Nellie, the Judge's justice is a series of acts, a bit of comedy followed by a bit of tragedy, each 'turn' followed by a break for the audience to visit the bar. Casting those who come before him in roles within the play according to his mood, this bitterly farcical figure takes a particular delight in gently passing his verdict on the sweet youth, Sonny, whose crime has been to ride a horse into Vinegaroon: 'Time will pass, and seasons will come and go. Soon, summer with her shimmering heatwaves on the baked horizon. Then, fall with her yellow harvest moon and the hills growing golden under the sinking sun . . . then winter with its biting, whining wind and the land mantled over white with snow . . . and finally – spring again with its waving green grass, and heaps of sweet-smelling flowers on every hill. . . . BUT YOU WON'T BE HERE TO SEE NONE OF THEM!'

In returning to the form after nearly a decade, Boetticher has evidently wanted to contemporize his style, to keep abreast of where the western has been. Hence the slight flexing of muscles with the zoomar lens, the slowing of action at key moments. But this last in particular is evidence of a thoughtfulness on Boetticher's part; often he has suggested the innocence of a Lumière in allowing the interested audience a careful view of the West's small dramas, the pulling out of a wagon from mud, the nursing of a sick animal, the rodeo. Neither do the traces of Peckinpah in the film, nor its air of being a conservative parable about youth and violence, detract from its quality: *A Time for Dying* has more to do, of course, with *The Cimarron Kid* (where it is a young Audie Murphy who is disillusioned by the world) than either *Ride the High Country* or Berkeley.

The flaw in this fine film lies elsewhere. Boetticher's great quality has always been his narrative power, in particular his realization of strong characters, a firm foundation on which he could play creatively. *A Time for Dying*, as with *Two Mules for Sister Sara* (which was also scripted while in Mexico), departs sharply from Boetticher's traditional terrain in concentrating on a *love* story. And the film fails finally because its quirky hero and the surprisingly hard Nellie at the centre of the action never truly marry. The looseness flows less from its cameoed villains than from the failure of its heart to come alive; *The Tall T* is deeply moving because we *care* if Boone dies.

Boetticher has had two careers thus far. However he proceeds, the great Ranown pictures and the original, distinctive *Arruza* comprise a substantial achievement. We must not be surprised if his progress through the third cycle of his work proves, like that of his characters, a chequered one. A man who lives so fully out of a personal style will have his highs and lows. Much may well depend on whether Boetticher can build a strong team on which he can draw, a pattern already again emerging. But either way, Boetticher will demand, and deserve, our attention.

Filmography: Budd Boetticher

Filmography compiled by Chris Wicking

Oscar Boetticher Junior – known as Budd – was born in Chicago, Illinois, on 29 July 1916. He studied at Ohio State University. He was sent to Mexico to recover from the effects of taking part in the American football season, and there became interested in bullfighting; he was the pupil of Lorenzo Garza, then a professional matador. He was taken on as technical adviser for the Mamoulian remake of *Blood and Sand* (1941); then, having been a messenger-boy for a while at Hal Roach's studios, he became an assistant director on: *Destroyer* (William A. Seiter, 1943); *The More The Merrier* (George Stevens, 1943); *The Desperadoes* (Charles Vidor, 1943); *Cover Girl* (Charles Vidor, 1944); and, in 1944, co-directed two other films with Lew Landers and William Berke (titles unknown).

Films directed by Boetticher:

1944 *One Mysterious Night, The Missing Juror, Youth on Trial*
1945 *A Guy, A Gal and a Pal, Escape in the Fog*
1946 Several propaganda films for the U.S. Armed Forces, one of which, *The Fleet that Came to Stay*, had commercial distribution
1948 *Assigned to Danger, Behind Locked Doors*
1949 *Black Midnight, Wolf Hunters*
1950 *Killer Shark*
1951 *The Bullfighter and the Lady, The Sword of d'Artagnan* (made as the pilot show for a TV series, it subsequently had commercial distribution. Boetticher shot it in three days), *The Cimarron Kid*
1952 *Bronco Buster, Red Ball Express, Horizons West*
1953 *City Beneath the Sea, Seminole, The Man from the Alamo, Wings of the Hawk, East of Sumatra*
1955 *The Magnificent Matador, The Killer is Loose*

Between 1955 and 1960 Boetticher made a number of television programmes: the pilot show for *Maverick*, with Jack Kelly; four episodes of *The Dick Powell Show* (30 mins. each); *The Count of Monte-Cristo* (60 mins.); *Captain Cat* (episode of the series *Hong Kong*, with Rod Taylor and Herbert Marshall)

1956 *Seven Men from Now*
1957 *The Tall T, Decision at Sundown*
1958 *Buchanan Rides Alone*
1959 *Ride Lonesome, Westbound*
1960 *Comanche Station, The Rise and Fall of Legs Diamond*
1959–68 *Arruza*
1969 *A Time for Dying*
Boetticher also wrote the original script of *Two Mules for Sister Sara.*

Westerns
The Cimarron Kid (1951)

Production Company	Universal-International
Producer	Ted Richmond
Director	Budd Boetticher
Script	Louis Stevens
Director of Photography	Charles P. Boyle
Colour Process	Technicolor
Editor	Frank Gross
Art Directors	Bernard Herzbrun, Emrich Nicholson
Musical Director	Joseph Gershenson

Audie Murphy (*Cimarron Kid*), Beverly Tyler (*Carrie Roberts*), John Hudson (*Dynamite Dick*), James Best (*Bitter Creek*), Leif Erickson (*Marshal Sutton*), Noah Beery, Jnr (*Bob Dalton*).

Running time: 83 mins.
Distributor: G.F.D.
First shown in Britain in 1953.

Bronco Buster (1952)

Production Company	Universal-International
Producer	Ted Richmond
Director	Budd Boetticher
Script	Horace McCoy, Lillie Hayward, based on a story by Peter B. Kyne
Director of Photography	Clifford Stine
Colour Process	Technicolor
Editor	Edward Curtiss
Art Directors	Bernard Herzbrun, Robert Boyle
Musical Director	Joseph Gershenson

John Lund (*Tom Moody*), Scott Brady (*Bart Eaton*), Joyce Holden (*Judy Bream*), Chill Wills (*Dan Bream*), Don Haggerty (*Dobie*), Dan Poore (*Elliot*), Casey Tibbs, Pete Crump, Manuel Enos, Jerry Spangler (*Themselves*).

Running time: 80 mins.
Distributor: G.F.D.

Horizons West (1952)

Production Company	Universal-International
Producer	Albert J. Cohen
Director	Budd Boetticher
Script	Louis Stevens
Director of Photography	Charles P. Boyle
Colour Process	Technicolor
Editor	Ted J. Kent
Art Directors	Bernard Herzbrun, Robert Clatworthy
Musical Director	Joseph Gershenson

Robert Ryan (*Dan Hammond*), Julia Adams (*Lorna Hardin*), Rock Hudson (*Neal Hammond*), John McIntyre (*Ira Hammond*), Judith Braun (*Sally Eaton*), Raymond Burr (*Cord Hardin*), Dennis Weaver (*Dandy Taylor*), Frances Bavier (*Martha Hammond*).

Running time: 81 mins.
Distributor: G.F.D.

Seminole (1953)

Production Company	Universal-International
Producer	Howard Christie
Director	Budd Boetticher
Script	Charles K. Peck, Jnr
Director of Photography	Russell Metty
Colour Process	Technicolor
Editor	Virgil Vogel
Art Directors	Alexander Golitzen, Emrich Nicholson
Musical Director	Joseph Gershenson

Rock Hudson (*Lt Caldwell*), Barbara Hale (*Revere Muldoon*), Anthony Quinn (*Osceola*), Richard Carlson (*Major Degan*), Hugh O'Brien (*Kajeck*), Russell Johnson (*Lt Hamilton*), Lee Marvin (*Sgt Magruder*).

Running time: 86 mins.
Distributor: G.F.D.

The Man from the Alamo (1953)

Production Company	Universal-International
Producer	Aaron Rosenberg
Director	Budd Boetticher
Script	Steve Fisher, D. D. Beauchamp
Director of Photography	Russell Metty
Colour Process	Technicolor
Editor	Virgil Vogel

| Art Directors | Alexander Golitzen, Emrich Nicholson |
| Music | Frank Skinner |

Glenn Ford (*John Stroud*), Julia Adams (*Beth Anders*), Chill Wills (*John Gage*), Hugh O'Brien (*Lt Lamar*), Victor Jory (*Jess Wade*), Neville Brand (*Dawes*), John Day (*Cavish*).

Running time: 79 mins.
Distributor: G.F.D.

Wings of the Hawk (1953)

Production Company	Universal-International
Producer	Aaron Rosenberg
Director	Budd Boetticher
Script	James E. Moser
Director of Photography	Clifford Stine
Editor	Russell Schoengarth
Art Directors	William Herzbrun, Robert Clatworthy
Music	Frank Skinner

Van Heflin ('*Irish*' *Gallagher*), Julia Adams (*Raquel*), George Dolen (*Col Ruiz*), Pedro Gonzales-Gonzales (*Tomas*), Rodolfo Acosta (*Arturo*), Antonio Moreno (*Father Perez*), Abbe Lane (*Elena*).

Running time: 80 mins.
Distributor: G.F.D.
First shown in Britain in 1954.

Seven Men from Now (1956)

Production Company	Batjac
Producers	Andrew V. McLaglen, Robert E. Morrison
Director	Budd Boetticher
Script	Burt Kennedy
Director of Photography	William H. Clothier
Colour Process	WarnerColor
Editor	Everett Sutherland
Art Director	Leslie Thomas
Music	Henri Vars
Sound	Earl Crain, Jnr

Randolph Scott (*Ben Stride*), Gail Russell (*Annie*), Lee Marvin (*Masters*), Walter Reed (*John Greer*), John Larch (*Pate Bodeen*), Donald Barry (*Clete*).

Running time: 77 mins.
Distributor: Warner Brothers.
First shown in Britain in 1957.

The Tall T (1957)

Production Company	Scott-Brown Productions
Producer	Harry Joe Brown
Director	Budd Boetticher
Script	Burt Kennedy, based on a story by Elmore Leonard
Director of Photography	Charles Lawton, Jnr
Colour Process	Technicolor
Editor	Al Clark
Art Director	George Brooks
Music conducted by	Mischa Bakaleinikoff
Sound	Ferol Redd

Randolph Scott (*Pat Brennan*), Richard Boone (*Usher*), Maureen O'Sullivan (*Doretta Mims*), Arthur Hunnicutt (*Ed Rintoon*), Skip Homeier (*Billy Jack*), Henry Silva (*Chink*), John Hubbard (*Willard Mims*), Robert Burton (*Tenvoorde*).

Running time: 77 mins.
Distributor: Columbia.

Decision at Sundown (1957)

Production Company	Scott-Brown Productions
Producer	Harry Joe Brown
Director	Budd Boetticher
Script	Charles Lang, Jnr, from a story by Vernon L. Fluharty
Director of Photography	Burnett Guffey
Colour Process	Technicolor
Editor	Al Clark
Art Director	Robert Peterson
Music	Heinz Roemheld
Sound	Jean Valentino

Randolph Scott (*Bart Allison*), John Carroll (*Tate Kimbrough*), Karen Steele (*Lucy Summerton*), Valerie French (*Ruby James*), Noah Beery, Jnr (*Sam*), John Archer (*Doctor Storrow*), Andrew Duggan (*Sheriff Swede Hansen*).

Running time: 77 mins.
Distributor: Columbia.
First shown in Britain 1958.

Buchanan Rides Alone (1958)

Production Company	Scott-Brown Productions
Producer	Harry Joe Brown
Associate Producer	Randolph Scott

Director	Budd Boetticher
Script	Charles Lang, from the novel *The Name's Buchanan*, by Jonas Ward
Director of Photography	Lucien Ballard
Colour Process	Columbia Colour
Art Director	Robert Boyle
Sound	John Livadary, Jean Valentino

Randolph Scott (*Buchanan*), Craig Stevens (*Abe Carbo*), Barry Kelley (*Lew Agry*), Tol Avery (*Simon Agry*), Peter Whitney (*Amos Agry*), Manuel Rojas (*Juan*).

Running time: 77 mins.
Distributor: Columbia.
First shown in Britain in 1959.

Ride Lonesome (1959)

Production Company	Ranown/Columbia
Executive Producer	Harry Joe Brown
Producer/Director	Budd Boetticher
Script	Burt Kennedy
Director of Photography	Charles Lawton, Jnr (filmed in CinemaScope)
Colour Process	Eastman Colour
Editor	Jerome Thomas
Art Director	Robert Peterson
Music	Heinz Roemheld
Sound	John Livadary, Harry Mills

Randolph Scott (*Ben Brigade*), Karen Steele (*Carrie*), Pernell Roberts (*Sam Boone*), James Best (*Billy John*), Lee Van Cleef (*Frank*), James Coburn (*Wid*), Dyke Johnson (*Charlie*), Boyd Stockman (*Indian Chief*).

Running time: 73 mins.
Distributor: Columbia.

Westbound (1959)

Production Company	Warner Brothers
Producer	Henry Blanke
Director	Budd Boetticher
Script	Berne Giler, Albert Shelby LeVino
Director of Photography	J. Peverell Marley
Colour Process	WarnerColor
Editor	Philip W. Anderson
Art Director	Howard Campbell
Music	David Buttloph
Sound	Sam Goode

136

Randolph Scott (*John Hayes*), Virginia Mayo (*Norma Putnam*), Karen Steele (*Jeannie Miller*), Michael Dante (*Red Miller*), Andrew Duggan (*Clay Putnam*), Michael Pate (*Mace*), Wally Brown (*Stubby*).

Running time: 69 mins.
Distributor: Warner Brothers.

Comanche Station (1960)

Production Company	Ranown
Executive Producer	Harry Joe Brown
Producer/Director	Budd Boetticher
Script	Burt Kennedy
Director of Photography	Charles Lawton, Jnr (filmed in CinemaScope)
Colour Process	Technicolor (Eastman Colour Print by Pathé)
Editor	Edwin Bryant
Art Director	Carl Anderson
Music Director	Mischa Bakaleinikoff
Sound	George Cooper
Sound Recordist	John Livadary

Randolph Scott (*Jefferson Cody*), Nancy Gates (*Mrs Lowe*), Claude Akins (*Ben Lane*), Skip Homeier (*Frank*), Richard Rust (*Dobie*).

Running time: 73 mins.
Distributor: Columbia.

A Time For Dying (1969)

Production Company	Fipco
Producer	Audie Murphy
Director	Budd Boetticher
Script	Budd Boetticher
Director of Photography	Lucien Ballard
Colour Process	Eastman Colour
Editor	Harry Knapp
Art Director	Leslie Thomas
Music	Harry Betts
Sound	John Carter

Richard Lapp (*Cass Bunning*), Anne Randall (*Nellie Winters*), Bob Randon (*Billy Pimple*), Victor Jory (*Judge Roy Bean*), Audie Murphy (*Jesse James*).

Running time: 90 mins.

4: Sam Peckinpah: the Savage Eye

Given his stormy career and modest output, a definitive analysis of Peckinpah's films seems both difficult and unwise. Ironically, Peckinpah has not suffered the near-total neglect of the older men. Yet interpretation of his work which has been advanced seems to me to have undervalued it. If nothing else, an interim study, proceeding through an analysis of the individual films, seems called for, especially since the distinctive qualities of his work in the form demand attention within the structure of this book.

To take the full measure of the man, we must begin with *Major Dundee*. One of Hollywood's great broken monuments, the film is a contemporary landmark in the western. With characteristic audacity, Peckinpah in his third film attacked an epic theme of such deep personal significance that his career itself was to be thrown into jeopardy. That the film as it stands now is not easily accessible to general audiences may be true, although not, in my view, self-evident given the crippling lack of faith and salesmanship that has characterized its exhibition. But either way, this does nothing to excuse the total neglect of this important picture by criticism.

The film was to be up to an hour longer than it is at present. Although trimmed and truncated throughout, it lost important scenes or major sequences which can be briefly described here:

(1) The film was to open with B Troop, having failed to locate Sierra Charriba after two months of tracking him, *en route* to the Rostes ranch where they join in a Halloween party. These scenes, which were to be

shot last and as a result were never shot at all, would establish Ryan (our narrator) and Beth Rostes who enjoy a brief flirtation, Lt Brannin, the scout Riago, the Rostes and their younger children, one or two of whom scurry about dressed as Apache.

(2) Then the real Indians come. The massacre, a long and violent one, was omitted because the producer could not accept an opening that postponed the introduction of the major characters for twenty to thirty minutes. Its absence works to heighten the obsessional quality of Dundee's pursuit of the Apache.

(3) In returning to Fort Benlin from the scene of the massacre Dundee and C Troop recapture Tyreen, the Hadley brothers, Jimmy Lee Benteen and Sgt Chillum, the manacled Confederates caught in a stream as they flee the jail. A brief exchange between Dundee and Sgt Gomez establishes the latter as one who as a boy had been stolen by the Apache and had ridden with them for two years against his fellow Mexicans.

(4) After Jimmy Lee Benteen's baiting of Aesop, a scene where Dundee breaks out the whisky as a compliment to the men on their conduct crossing the river. Two toasts are made, one by Sgt Chillum to the Confederacy, the other by the preacher, Dahlstrom, to the Union, which results in the whole command spilling their whisky except the mulepacker, Wiley.

(5) As the command moves out to the Mexican village after the river ambush, a long scene where the men fall about laughing hysterically, but *silently*, as Dundee tries in vain to get the mule he is mounted on to move.

(6) Footage from the night of the *fiesta* including a drunken scene where Dundee and Tyreen relive their West Point days, and a knife-fight between Potts and Gomez, half-serious and half-staged, the two men expressing a kind of love in their testing of each other, the crowd of soldiers and Mexicans watching admiringly until Dundee breaks it up revealing himself as the outsider, only he not understanding.

(7) Scenes of Dundee's breakdown and drunken wanderings in Durango, including a long montage of his memories of all that has happened. Also, drunken moments of pleasure between Gomez and Potts as Tyreen rescues Dundee.

(8) The discovery of Riago's mutilated corpse strapped to a tree by the Apache, Potts insisting that Dundee himself cut down the scout whose loyalty he has doubted throughout.

Within this perspective it is clear that what we have in the released version is a severely damaged work which Peckinpah himself can only look back on with pain and misgivings. However, for all this, in my view the power and meaning are still there, the structure

Sam Peckinpah shooting *The Wild Bunch*

and imagery clear, the deeply personal statement of the film undeniable.

Peckinpah is fond of describing the thematic continuity of his work in terms of a preoccupation with losers (a TV play he produced and directed was called *The Losers*), misfits and drifters. Certainly, the work of few directors is so peopled with characters who are emotionally, spiritually or physically *crippled*. However, more precisely, Peckinpah's characters suffer from not knowing who they are: above all, it is the quest for personal identity that provides the dramatic action of his films, a quest seen both in terms of a meaningful confrontation or dialogue with the past, and a tortured struggle to achieve mastery over self-annihilating and *savage* impulses. In *Major Dundee* these themes inform the conflict of jailer and jailed, of Dundee and Tyreen, two characters who share a troubled history and an uncertainty about their role. Tyreen has been three men – Irish immigrant, cashiered Union

officer (Dundee casting the deciding vote), Confederate rebel – and now stands or falls by the romanticism of his posture, that of the complete cavalier. The style is there in his first appearance, where Dundee asks for volunteers from the Confederate prisoners to join the band he is assembling to pursue the Apache. In torch-lit darkness we see the manacled figure – arms crossed and head low, a martyred Christ – as he makes his noble gesture: 'It's not my country, Major. I damn its flag and I damn you. And I would rather hang than serve!' A feather cocked in his cap, Tyreen remains true to the style throughout (Richard Harris has been much maligned for giving his best performance here): in his fanciful encounters with Senta Berger's Teresa, in his perverse refusal to break his promise to Dundee (his enemy at both private and military levels), in his personal execution of O. W. Hadley, one of his men who has deserted. Although Tyreen insists often and rhetorically that he will serve only until the Apache are taken or destroyed, the confusions inherent in his position trap him fatally. In the final battle with the French Lancers it is the gallant Tyreen who is mortally wounded saving the hated Union colours when they fall, then dying grotesquely in a single-handed charge against the lances of two hundred French reinforcements. Recalling the passing of Steve Judd in *Ride the High Country*, Tyreen dies the way he lived, in a magnificently romantic gesture which undoubtedly has its usefulness; the French charge broken, Dundee and the few survivors slip into Texas and safety.

Having fought 'his own war' at Gettysburg, Major Amos Charles Dundee now finds himself a jailer as the struggle between North and South rages on. His obsessive pursuit of Sierra Charriba also soon takes on the quality of a private war. In general, Peckinpah's heroes are complex, paradoxical figures. Moral rectitude – originally the very quality that shaped the traditional heroes of the genre – is often what they *suffer* from, characters so committed to living by the book that they seek to embody its very *spirit*. It is the ideal of perfection, the sense of being *the elect*, that can animate a Peckinpah hero, the power of the protagonist rooted less in ethical considerations than in something akin to a metaphysical imperative.

In so far as they can break free of their righteousness to a sense of their own imperfection, Peckinpah's characters can grow and achieve self-knowledge. But if – like Dundee and his forbear of *Ride the High Country*, Joshua Knudsen – they do not, they are trapped in a destructive pattern ever moving from the peaks of judgement to the troughs of guilt. Before he is through, the Major, not a pretty character, decimates his command, destroys a Mexican village, provokes a war with neutral French forces, and leaves a bloody trail of death and destruction stretching far behind him.

The pursuit of the Apache can resolve nothing for Dundee, since it functions as a headlong escape from placing his own house in order. The Major himself seems to hint at this when Teresa, the Austrian widow, asks him why men must for ever be fighting: 'War is simple . . . men can understand it.' Women are important to Peckinpah: where they know who *they* are and what their role is, they can positively assist in men's search for understanding and equilibrium. Here Teresa, a mature and sophisticated woman, freely gives herself to Dundee because she wants to feel alive, to escape the destruction that is everywhere. This gift exposes Dundee – the Major, breaking with the book, has gone beyond his own pickets to make love by a languid pool – and forces upon him the fact of his own fallibility. Betraying the woman, Dundee spirals into a sodden purgatory to land in the garbage of the streets of Durango. Wallowing in his guilt, it is the Major's turn to play the fallen Christ, the swing of the pendulum elevating Tyreen who now goads him back into action. Ironically, earlier the Major had pronounced on the Lieutenant: 'He is corrupt . . . but I will save him.'

Although Tyreen is ever there to accuse him and force a self-awareness – when Dundee compulsively buries his dead after the Indian ambush, at the pool with Teresa, in the gutters of Durango – the Major is finally trapped within his idea of himself. Less of the elect than of *the damned*, Dundee can find no peace or freedom in his crusade to 'smite the wicked'. When Sierra Charriba and his warriors have been laid low, Dundee and Tyreen again confront each other only to be interrupted by the attack of the French. Their dialogue unresolved, Tyreen falls in the fighting, and the Major survives to carry on with his own war. The final image is a disquieting one, the bloody remnants of the command pushing on into the cactus-dominated prairie.

This account of action at the level of character makes *Major Dundee* sound more coherent than it is. Even if we allow for the elisions resulting from extensive production cuts, the narrative remains deeply disturbing in the twists and turns with which it develops. To gain a grip on *Major Dundee* as a whole and extend the levels of meaning that I have been discussing, it is necessary to attend to the total conception of the work, one of immense ambition and intelligence. For here Peckinpah explores his themes within a framework that mounts to a monumental attempt to lay bare the roots of America as a nation: the quest for personal identity is anchored in, and informed by, the parallel and overriding theme of national definition. Ever in the background of the great epic painting that *Major Dundee* resembles is the Civil War; and the confusions that both its principal characters face are rooted in that background and of a peculiarly American nature. Dundee, a man of Southern birth, has turned on his own kind to fight for the North, an act clearly in accord with the legalistic character of the man. Tyreen, the Irish potato-farmer and former Union officer, has joined the rebels.

These contradictions are reflected in the force that Dundee assembles to pursue the Apache. Settlers and renegades, Union soldiers, Confederate prisoners and Negroes tired of sweeping stables, horse-thief and preacher, veteran Indian scout and innocent bugle-boy, inexperienced lieutenant of artillery and Mexican sergeant at home with the Apache, the anomalies and divisions of early America are starkly evoked here. As they ride out and Dundee asks Ryan for a tune, the Confederates strike up 'Dixie', the bluecoats respond with 'The Battle Hymn of the Republic', and the civilians bring up the rear with 'My Darling Clementine'. If the snatches of this last point to Ford's film (which Peckinpah admires) it is more than appropriate: although the vision here is tragic rather than pastoral, a dance of death rather than a wedding, the films belong to the same tradition, stretching back through *Union Pacific*,

The Iron Horse, The Covered Wagon, to *Birth of a Nation* itself. Given this genealogy and the film's structure, it is right that the threat emerges in racial terms: 'You're forgetting your manners, nigger.' Temporary solidarity vanishes when Jimmy Lee Benteen taunts Aesop, the command instantly splitting into opposed camps. The force stays together only because the impulse to savage each other is held in uneasy check and given other outlets. '*Until the Apache are taken or destroyed.*' Ringing out like an incantation in the film, the phrase takes on greater significance in this context. For if Dundee can only define himself through his righteous mission, his command, like the new nation itself, is only held together by a single-minded drive to destroy the common enemy. Led by tortured men at the mercy of self-annihilating impulses, the crazy-quilt company wheels blindly, slowly acquiring a shared past, a bloody one, gradually achieving definition as a group, if not identity. At this level the real action of *Major Dundee* is the freezing of the command in a barbaric posture, and this Peckinpah communicates brilliantly.

It is in these terms that the movement of the film, concentric rather than linear, must be seen. At the fort we enjoy a comfortable relationship with the familiar situation of an ambitious officer with a shady past, the prospect of a pursuit of Indians who have taken hostages. The crisp pace here, together with Charlton Heston's authoritative Dundee, naturally arouses expectations in us of action that will have purpose and direction. However, once away from the fort all this is gradually but totally undercut by a series of dislocations so disturbing that they have the effect, finally, of giving *Major Dundee* the air of a bitterly artful parody of the traditional cavalry picture. The recurrent features of this form are familiar: an undermanned company (or settlement), while torn by internal conflicts, functions as the heroic unit in achieving the group objective, the defeat of the faceless hostile. If the form has been brilliantly inflected by both Ford and Mann (*Fort Apache, The Last Frontier*) to make deeply ambiguous statements, nowhere has it been so relentlessly undermined as in Peckinpah's hands. Pushing the structure to its breaking-point, Peckinpah both stresses the

Major Dundee: the pursuit of the Apache, and crossing the river

divisive tensions within the group and renders the objective wholly meaningless except in so far as it serves to channel savage impulses. By placing the defeat of the Apache immediately prior to the French attack, Peckinpah makes of it a minor climax, compressing the action into a relentless barrage shot head-on largely from middle distance, the total effect being to create an odd vacuum at its end.

The presence of the French is a particularly disturbing element. Just *what*, we wonder, are they doing down there, in Mexico, in this movie? Yet the structure of *Major Dundee* demands their presence since it is the challenge they pose – at the United States border – which makes clear the identity that Dundee and his men have achieved in their pursuit and extermination of the Indians: that of *Americans*. Once across the river Dundee will again ask his bugler for a tune and this time, as the picture ends, there will be no war of opposing melodies. Peckinpah takes great care to establist the French, with their colourful uniforms and martial sense, as a force that carries traditions and a past, a distinct identity, thus highlighting the primitiveness of the Americans. When Dundee threatens an attack on the French garrison at the Mexican village and its commander replies that international law is being breached, Sam Potts, the scout bearing the ultimatum, stolidly replies: 'The Major ain't no lawyer, Sonny.'

'But who do you answer to . . .?' Dundee's shortcomings, his compulsion and lack of self-knowledge, are pointed within the structure of the film through Michael Anderson Jnr's humble Ryan and Jim Hutton's bumpkinish Lt Graham. Growing in stature as the film progresses, it is Graham who holds the command together when Dundee breaks. On the night of the *fiesta* where both Tyreen and Dundee, the prisoners of their styles, waltz with Teresa, Graham interrupts to join the woman in a wild and exciting Mexican dance. It is Ryan, on the other hand, whose sensible diary of the events is used as a commentary throughout, an ambitious device Peckinpah employs both to distance us further from the action (as with the assault of the film's violence) and to give the work the appropriate tone of a chronicle. Ryan also has a relationship of great warmth and simplicity with a Mexican girl – kissing her good-bye sleepily before the whole company until the Major orders him to 'put it in the saddle!' – which acts as a foil to the impotent Dundee/Teresa affair. But in spite of all this, and the fact that it is Ryan (who has a *personal* score to settle with Charriba since he alone escaped the massacre) who destroys the Apache chief and not Dundee, neither of these characters finally emerge as substantial positive alternatives. Simply put, the two men strike us as *innocent*. It is difficult to believe that either has a past, that the securing of a mature identity that Peckinpah insists on does not lie before them. If these men have made a beginning, they have yet to travel through the terrain upon which all of Peckinpah's heroes live, the struggle with destructive impulses out of which independent and meaningful action can come.

In *Major Dundee* this struggle is embodied in the complex interaction of Indian and white man, a key motif woven through the fabric of the film with great skill. Treating the Apache in a ghostly and ritualistic way, Peckinpah creates them both as an objective evil and as a savage direction open to all men – an interior potential. Thus the effect of the brutal Apache massacre, the aftermath of which opens the film, is balanced by the cavalry's eventual liquidation of the Indians, the inhuman treatment of the Mexicans by the French, their exploitation by the Americans, and, last but not least, the butchery of the end. The structure is made morally complex by the historical fact, insisted on, that the Apache have some justification – 'It's their land . . . all of it' – which places in perspective the 'civilized' behaviour of both Old World and New. Peckinpah underlines the moral ambiguity by his use of costumes which function ingeniously as *masks* throughout the film. Lean, brown and breech-clouted, the Rostes boys return to hum happily as they demonstrate their skill with bow and arrow. Moments later, Tyreen only barely saves himself as he reconnoitres the river from Apache disguised as Union soldiers by realizing the trick when they fail to respond to his whistled 'Dixie'. Although they don Mexican clothes from time to time, the command itself become increasingly like the Apache as the film progresses, a fact underlined by the trap that is finally sprung on the Indians, together with the bloodiness of the final river battle. This complex interplay is extended structurally through the rituals that recur in the film (the Halloween party that was never shot, the Christmas Eve gathering in the ruins, the *fiesta*) and which are ever the prelude to slaughter, the two rites brought together in the final battle, savage, gory, but a *celebration* of violence none the less.

At the heart of the ideological structure of *Major Dundee* are three key characters, none of whom are simply Americans. There is Riago, who says disgustedly of himself that he is no longer an Apache, like Charriba, but a *Christian* Indian; and there is Mario Adorf's Sgt Gomez, a Mexican who functions with the skills of an Indian: both of these characters suffer as a result of cuts. But paramountly, there is Sam Potts. In trying to elicit an understated performance from James Coburn (in which he clearly succeeded), Peckinpah is said to have told the actor repeatedly that he was playing a *pro*. However, in terms of my analysis, it would be more accurate to say that Potts is the one character at Dundee's own level who knows who he is and what his role is. A figure of resolute independence and intelligent detachment ('Everyone else seems to be doing it', he remarks when Dundee wonders why an Indian should turn against his own people), the character is vital to Dundee, ever pointing his direction. But where others in the party serve out of inner compulsion, blind allegiance, the threat of execution, Potts has the capacity for choice. Hence the strange power of that amusing moment when Potts and Riago entertain the camp on Christmas Eve with a 'high-spirited, brotherly bout of wrestling' (a moment that would have been reinforced by the knife-fight between Potts and Gomez at the *fiesta*, now cut). Part of the scene's quality comes from our awareness of how appropriate this savage fight is as entertainment for the command, since it is a parody of the instincts they hold towards each other. But more than this, what is striking – for the command as well as us – is that we are watching men secure enough in themselves to be able to *choose* violence as a mode of behaviour, an expression of feeling.

Sam Potts is crucial to an understanding of Sam Peckinpah. A kind of half-breed, a squaw-man, a man of the mountains, Potts, like the apocryphal Daniel Boone or Bill Cody, stands between savagery and civilization. Indeed, within the figure this dialectic comes to rest, its marriage shielding the character from the destructive righteousness of a Dundee, the nihilistic romanticism of a Tyreen. But history, in Peckinpah's view, is not made by those who have found their personal salvation. The tragedy of *Major Dundee* is that the whole man is a *cripple*, that the one-armed scout, serene and aloof (wholly so from Teresa), is finally almost irrelevant, an observer and an accomplice in actions springing from the tortured soul of Dundee, caught fast in his private limbo and yet dictating the course of events, the blood-bath from which America is born.

The Deadly Companions and *Ride the High Country*

Major Dundee takes pride of place in this study for its accurate description of the contours of Peckinpah's world. This perspective of a double vision at once historical and metaphysical, the individual both located within a continuing society and stretched on the rack of a spiritual quest, immediately makes clear why Peckinpah has been so dismissive of *The Deadly Companions*, his strange and impressive début as a Hollywood director. Ideal for a Mann or a Boetticher, A. S. Fleischmann's property flows wholly from the archetypal base of the genre, a psychological revenge fable that describes a demonic wasteland through which its haunted characters move. Restrained from doing more than tinker with the script, Peckinpah left the picture after the first cut and has since dubbed it an 'unworkable project', surprisingly cavalier given how much of himself he got into the film. Criticism has been too quick to take him at his word, tacitly honouring a simplistic conception of the relationship between film-maker, material and system. A serious director will always crave total freedom stretching from the script through the final cut to embrace even the sales campaign. But if a director is one whose ancestors were pioneers (and perhaps Indians), who learned Biblical verse in his childhood from his father, a rancher and a judge, surely we must ask what greater freedom – in the *first* place – can he have than the opportunity just to make westerns?

The Deadly Companions is an astonishing first film, Peckinpah wholly dominating the material and overcoming the considerable problems of odd psychological elements (the scar and powerless shooting arm of the hero, the coffin, the ghost town), some weak dialogue, and a shortage of physical action. If he himself looks back on the film as a compromise, given its a-historical world, nothing is more revealing for the critic than *how* a director compromises. But whatever Peckinpah may say, *The Deadly Companions* could not but have involved him imaginatively given its movement of a journey into the past, its theme of the interior struggle with the temptations of savagery. Treating the psychological elements lightly (only the scar now mars the film) and evoking an infernal landscape, Peckinpah creates the action of a spiritual odyssey, Yellowleg and Kit Tilden deeply troubled characters driven to redeem themselves and establish secure identity.

As they move into the arid, cactus-ridden Apache country, Peckinpah locates the party within the CinemaScope frame precisely, underlining the conflicts at work. The angry Kit sits alone on her buckboard with its sad cargo, while the man who has accidentally killed her son rides alongside in earnest dialogue with her. Hanging on behind are the jeering Billy and Turk, figures out of their past, waiting like vultures for their prey. In obsessively driving on to bury Mead by the dead husband that Gila City has never believed in, Kit is trying to break free of her brutalized life. An early darker version of Tyreen, Steve Cochran's Billy is all style and bravado, ever ready to manhandle the woman and reduce her to an animal, keeping him at bay with a rock. Successful as this figure is, Chill Wills's Turk is on a different plane altogether, a gross shambling barbarian decked out in buffalo coat and Indian beads, constantly rubbing up against buildings and cactus. The richness of this character goes a long way towards evoking Yellowleg's dilemma, to rid himself of the seven-year obsession to scalp the man who all but scalped him on a Civil War battlefield, without sacrificing what damaged sense of identity he has left, without himself spiralling down to the level of a savage.

However, this interior conflict is brilliantly objectified by Peckinpah in the latter, extraordinary half of the film. Once the villains have left the couple, the buckboard rounds a bend, and suddenly beyond it on a high crest a stagecoach is silhouetted against the sky driving full tilt and pursued by yelping Apache. The suddenness of the action, the distance, lighting and framing of the shot, are highly dislocating: what is happening? As the stage rolls down the hill to veer crazily round a pool before tipping over, we see that within it there are Indians garbed in shawls and bonnets, that the scene is a drunken parody of the action in which the stage was acquired. Peckinpah's realization is vigorous and intelligent, sharpening the bizarre quality that runs throughout the film, his personal edge giving the moment a disturbing complexity. Who is chasing whom? Who is Indian, who is white man? The shock we experience, the crisis of blurring lines between savage and civilized roles that the characters face, is then counterpointed in the mysterious struggle that we witness between Yellowleg and the lone Apache who now begins to haunt him, the ghostly figure trailing and teasing, a constant invitation to join in a violent duel.

However, if this were all, *The Deadly Companions* would not be the fine work that it is. The great achievement of the film is that while evoking the private conflict of its characters, it also describes a moving love-story. I use this sentimental phrase specifically to underline Peckinpah's resistance to the tug of psychological and archetypal drives in the script. Through Brian Keith (the fine actor whom Peckinpah had used as Dave Blassingame in his TV series, *The Westerner*) and Maureen O'Hara, Peckinpah makes good dramatically the *human* implications of the tensions within his characters. Frozen in a posture of righteousness, unable to give or take, Yellowleg and Kit tear at each other like animals. 'You don't know me well enough to hate me!' shouts Yellowleg when Kit lashes out at him with a whip. The slow and exhausting process by which the two come to know each other and themselves is finally the bedrock of the film, Peckinpah building on this action

153

surely to give flesh to his theme. Alone in a wild and primitive landscape, the man and woman gradually recognize their need, each other's humanity, and begin tentatively to reach out. The movement of the film (clearly looking forward to *Major Dundee*) whereby the characters progressively take on the appearance of Indians, the couple stolidly marching through the Apache country dragging their burden behind them on a *travois*, is finally broken with their arrival at Siringo and the delicate imagery of the woman picking flowers in a dusty corner of the ghost town, the man's face transformed by a rare smile. As Kit had layed Yellowleg's ghost to rest, blasting down the lone Apache when he wriggles into the cave to stand above her like a primeval spirit, so internal logic demands that Yellowleg destroy Billy, a meaningful symmetry that is absurdly withheld in the final cut. As the picture stands now it is Turk who kills his protégé, Peckinpah's ending altered, the director unlucky from the beginning.

American films have often described a love that is painfully earned: Maureen O'Hara perhaps reminds us of Ford's *Rio Grande*; we can look back as well to Howie and Lina of *The Naked Spur*. If we move further afield, there is no shortage of distinguished examples: Fuller's *Pick-up on South Street*, Kazan's *Wild River* are but two. Much rarer in the American cinema, however, are films that wed this action to a convincing process of *socialization*, evoking the pain of the individual forced to grow into an awareness of others, the animal becoming a social animal. Throughout the work of so many American film-makers there flows a deep stream of anarchy, a subversive current that insists that society is too oppressive, love is not possible, living with other people is not possible, community is not possible. In Peckinpah the anarchy is public and makes up one-half of the man, as with America itself, his continuing struggle with it objectified for us on the screen. In *Major Dundee* the battle is tragically lost; but in *The Deadly Companions*, Peckinpah's most optimistic work, it is painfully won.

There is no need to advance claims here for *Ride the High Country*; the great acclaim enjoyed by this work, so richly deserved has if anything obscured the consistency of Peckinpah's achievement. If *The Deadly Companions* can be seen as a pilgrimage, and *Major Dundee* as a crusade, *Ride the High Country* takes the form of a temptation. In all three films it is a dialogue that shapes the dramatic action, the structure here linking the two ageing ex-sheriffs who have begun to travel different roads in their response to a society which they helped to create and where they are now out of place. Falling on hard times for Gil Westrum has meant a surrender to forces destructive to his identity: a cheating side-show 'Oregon Kid', the pragmatic Westrum cheerfully caricatures himself, his red-bearded, Satanic cowboy a falsification and a denial of the past that he shares with Steve Judd. This old man, in contrast, clings desperately, and absurdly, to his past in a world of cops, horseless carriages and Chinese restaurants. Judd also has been damaged by the encroaching anonymity: pathetically tipping his hat to the noisy holiday crowd that awaits the spectacular race of horses and camel, the man has a bearing immeasurably above the frayed cuffs of his present, the bars and brothels of his immediate past. With the embattled pride has come a righteousness, a high sense of moral mission, and an obsession to honour all contracts. There is something very akin to desperation in the character's severity, his treatment of Westrum when the attempt on the gold is made. The bankers would not be hurt by the loss – 'Not them, only *me*!' shouts Judd, smiting the baser instinct before him. The temptation is confronted, disarmed and held – cruelly, we feel – in check: the companion of all those years makes the rest of the journey bound tightly.

Through his creation of key locations Peckinpah disturbingly evokes the forces that threaten meaningful existence. Once the party has left the world of balloons and belly-dancers that Westrum and his protégé, Heck, move through so easily, the action shifts to the Knudsen household. Through R. G. Armstrong, the brooding figure to which he was again to turn for *Major Dundee*'s Dahlstrom, Peckinpah creates one of his most impressive characters in Joshua, a dark, inward, finally incestuous figure whose response to the complexity and violence of the world has been to withdraw completely. The enemy of feeling and instinct, the Knudsen household is deeply repressive, the girl Elsa stunted and hiding herself in ill-fitting men's clothes, growth and self-knowledge finally impossible here. However, if both Westrum and Heck are cramped and out of place in this setting, Judd is not. 'My father says there's only right and wrong, good and evil, nothing in between. It isn't that simple, is it? – No, it isn't; it should be, but it isn't.' If the two characters are not cut from the same cloth, Judd, swapping proverb for proverb with Knudsen at the dinner-table, understands from first-hand the forces that drive the man. Peckinpah's great writing skill is perhaps at its peak in abuse: the end of the film where the Hammonds, 'red-necked pecker-woods . . . damn dry gulchin' Southern trash', are stung into defending their family honour openly is a typical example. But equally impressive is the mastery over prose with an Old Testament ring, here delicately linking Knudsen and Judd. 'Levity in the young is like unto a dry gourd with a seed rattling round inside.' Appropriately, Judd's own judgement earlier, if no less righteous, locates the character in time rather than absolute standards: 'Boys nowadays. No pride, no self-respect. Plenty of gall but no sand.'

The pastoral purity of the Knudsen farm and the overweening morality of its master faithfully delineate the spiritual centre of Steve Judd. In this context, the humbleness of his present task, the purgatorial quality of its movement from the home of self-righteousness to the Sodom and Gomorrah of Coarse Gold, and then painfully back, these are entirely correct. Just how mean the job is the party, increased by the fugitive Elsa, discover when they reach the mining camp. No grand sum here but a few thousand dollars, largely from the whorehouse that dominates the camp, as Kate points out, its real gold-mine. Balancing and complementing the Knudsen household, Coarse Gold is a brutish world of violence and excess. Instinct incarnate reigns supreme ('Have fun, Honey') as the lamb goes to the slaughter, Elsa joined to the Hammond brothers. In a world of moral grotesques and animals, it is Westrum who functions efficiently, unscrupulously destroying the judge's licence to marry so that the court must release Elsa. However, it is

Ride the High Country: the two gunfighters

Heck, seeing the girl as a person rather than an object, who prompts the act, Westrum forced to it to save his manpower for the attempt on the gold. With a cruel legalistic detachment ('the problem is you're legally married to Billy'), Judd himself continues rigidly committed to his own contract, prepared to accept the mining camp's justice even if it reduces Elsa to the status of an animal.

A network of detail, clustering round the figure of the girl, gives the action of *Ride the High Country* a delicate resonance. As she rides through the twilit camp at the head of her weird wedding procession, it is her mother's gown that she wears, the mother at whose grave Knudsen prays daily, its stone bearing the inscription: 'Wherefore O Harlot, I will judge thee as women that break wedlock and shed blood are judged. . . .' Marriage is a difficult business, life is complicated: Judge Tolliver, a man clearly broken by it all, knows: 'People change . . . the glory of a good marriage doesn't come in the beginning . . . it comes later on . . . it's hard work.' For Judd the commitment to a life of hard and good works has meant the sacrifice of home and family, the girl Sara Truesdale, whom Elsa resembles, left far behind to a comfortable life with a farmer, spawning grandchildren now. For the likes of Judd and Westrum history allowed no choice. Seen within this perspective, the character of Elsa is at the very centre of *Ride the High Country*, the soul of its action, her growth (the girl finally accepting a suitable costume) faithfully paralleling Judd's own progress. The delivery of the innocent from the savage forces that threaten her, the commitment to *her* value, these together with the redemption of Gil and Heck describe a rediscovery of a whole life.

With great vigour Peckinpah points the choices that men face through the deaths that await them. When the Hammond brothers attack, Sylvus circles up behind to find Heck waiting to shoot him brutally in the chest. Blasted down into a sitting position against a rock, Sylvus looks up uncomprehendingly as Heck takes the rifle and departs. Living on for a few seconds, the cold mountain wind sweeping over him, Sylvus sits there blinking and then pitches over to die in the dirt. It is a lonely death in a barren, savage place: barbarous and meaningless, it is the death of a wolf. The discovery of Knudsen's end is even more unsettling, Peckinpah playing tightly on the nervous hens who cluck in the barnyard adjoining the grave where the farmer prays, then cutting to zoom in from below on the bloody face, eyes frozen open and staring. The Hammonds revealed within the house, the violation of the hens by Henry's raven, these underscore our sense of the precariousness and inadequacy of Knudsen's stance in life, both a denial and celebration of death that has finally claimed its disciple.

At the end, we have the passing of Judd. Rising up from the ditch 'just like the old days', the partners face the struggle head-on and in the open. Like Christian soldiers they march into battle, Peckinpah cutting away to reveal the confusion in the animals that they face; then Judd is dying. Heck and Elsa, the future, are spared the pain of a good-bye, Westrum sadly taking his own farewell to leave the old man alone in the shadow of a great tree in the yard.

Ride the High Country: Elsa, 'the soul of the action'

Peckinpah frames the last shot with the greatest care, placing us directly behind Judd so that we share his last look away from the Knudsen household and out past the yellow and russet leaves of the forest to the far horizon, where the high country in all its savage majesty stands. Then Judd lies back and dies.

If nature is in affectionate sympathy at the end it is not because a god is dying: the elegiac tone of an autumnal world marks the passing of the old order. Like *Major Dundee* three years later, *Ride the High Country* is finally about America. The movement of the film describes not only a spiritual quest but a whole history as well ('that time in Lincoln County . . .'), a way of life torn between the ideals of a manifest moral destiny and the instincts of a pragmatic imperialism, a romanticized self-interest. Discussion of this great work has often erred in relegating the Scott figure to a secondary role, despite his magnificent charge, like the cavalry in early Ford, to join the party in the ditch, his equal place in the gunfight, his survival. But these two heroes, like Dundee and Tyreen, are masks for the same face, expressions of the same spirit, the spirit of the American West. Judd and Westrum, judge and cowboy, vision and violence, Peckinpah insists that both were necessary in a savage land.

The Wild Bunch

The characteristic quality that stamps Peckinpah's work is its disturbing edge. This is clearly evident even in much of Peckinpah's early television direction which deservedly has its own reputation. The surrealist jolt that so much of Peckinpah communicates flows from a particular way of seeing and experiencing the world. Luis Buñuel once observed that 'neo-realist reality is incomplete, official and altogether reasonable; but the poetry, the mystery, everything which completes and enlarges tangible reality is completely missing'. Different from Buñuel in many ways, Peckinpah nevertheless reveals a similarly all-embracing vision, a total response to the world. I am not suggesting direct influence here (although Peckinpah thinks *Los Olvidados*, the one Buñuel he has seen, a superb work); it is from Don Siegel, with whom he worked on a number of films starting with *Riot in Cell Block 11*, that Peckinpah originally learned most. However, Peckinpah's preoccupation with the existence of savage and destructive instincts, with the consequences of their repression or free play, and with the nightmarish struggle necessary before balance and identity can emerge, clearly anchors him in terrain that artists within the Surrealist movement have been traditionally concerned with.

The surrealist edge thus derives from Peckinpah's *realistic* world-view. In an increasingly liberal era, many American movies have underwritten the notion that evil resides not in our stars, nor ourselves, but in our environment. Peckinpah insists that men can be animals, that fate is inside us, that evil exists; that America's posture in the world, her power and menace, owe not a little to the existence of that evil. From the outset Peckinpah has resolutely demanded the material and conditions to make this personal statement. However, that he felt that he had been constrained from achieving his goal with *Major Dundee* is clear in his triumphant return to the cinema after nearly four years (given over to more TV, as with the remarkable *Noon Wine*, and to script-writing and planning) with what is a second and, on this occasion, completely realized *Major Dundee* in *The Wild Bunch*.

At the outset of this extraordinary work there is a shocking image which directly evokes the world that is to be explored. Scorpions struggle in a sea of killer ants, children gaily watching, as the Wild Bunch disguised as U.S. soldiers ride into Starbuck. While dramatically preparing us for the action that is to follow, the image also describes the relationship between Peckinpah's characters and the society through which they move. And we must not forget the children: above all, the moment introduces a network of detail that is crucial in the film, a structure in which innocence and cruelty, laughter and barbarity, idealism and blood-lust, exist side by side. Like birds on a string, children are part of a violent world. Especially in Mapache's Agua Verde Peckinpah insists on the point, a mother suckling her babe nestled between cartridge-belts, children riding the tortured body of Angel round the courtyard. In the final, indescribably bloody massacre, a small boy is gleefully a participator, shooting Pike Bishop in the back. The action here balances the opening, the hail of fire between bounty hunters and Bunch tearing the innocent ranks of the Temperance Union literally to bloody bits; and Peckinpah returns time and again to the children who are the massacre's spectators. Peckinpah's own small boy, Matthew, stands in the middle of it all, his arms round a little girl.

Within this perspective it is wholly appropriate that the action of *The Wild Bunch* is played out – once again – with civil war in the background. For it is the fathers, sons and brothers (the women too) of the same people who entertain the Bunch so gracefully in Angel's village, who eventually destroy Angel and his comrades. Man's twin capacities for love, joy and brotherhood, for destruction, lust and bestiality, is what *The Wild Bunch* – like all of Peckinpah's work – is finally about. And it is this central preoccupation that accounts for his abiding affinity for Mexico. Where

Boetticher responds to Mexico as an arena in which individualism still flourishes, Peckinpah loves it for its special place below the American waistline. If the United States has been quick to deny death and violence by institutionalizing them, to rob love of meaning by romanticizing it, Mexico (like Buñuel's Spain) shows little inclination to do either. Hence, in Mexican history and culture, Peckinpah finds action and ritual that he sees as *universally* significant in its candour. One measure of this is Peckinpah's respect for John Huston's *The Treasure of Sierra Madre* from which *The Wild Bunch* borrows so freely for its structure and the important character of Sykes. Hence too the emphasis in the film on ceremonies (invariably accompanied by richly evocative Mexican music) which Peckinpah creates as tribal rites, most notably the generous farewell of Angel's villagers to the Bunch, the funeral procession for Teresa, and finally the march of the Bunch itself to the slaughter at the end. The range of Mexican character that Peckinpah achieves is also relevant. The bird-like grace of Pike Bishop's prostitute is balanced by the toothy, carnivorous accountant of the *federales*; the gentle wisdom of the village elder who tries to teach Angel discipline is matched by the grotesque honour of Mapache who cuts his throat.

As Tector Gorch observes when the group are about to cross over: 'Just more of Texas as far as I'm concerned.' The world that Peckinpah creates is a continuous and morally complex one: Harrigan and the vulpine bounty hunters, the innocent U.S. Army recruits, the revolutionaries, the *federales*, the women and children, all have their roots in Peckinpah's metaphysical dialectic. However, as always, his vision forces a confrontation between what he feels to be essential drives in human nature, and the *social* costs of a failure to understand and control them. At the heart of the structure that I have been describing is the Wild Bunch itself; and Peckinpah's great achievement is to create these men both as a microcosm of the elements in conflict and as vividly particularized characters in time. The historical moment of the film is crucial: if *Ride the High Country* is an elegy on American individualism, if *Major Dundee* inquires into national identity, in *The Wild Bunch* it

The Wild Bunch: 'Let's go!'; 'Like birds on a string, children are part of a violent world'

is the male *group* that is Peckinpah's subject. Properly understood, the film is criticism: of the American idea of the male élite, of the professionalism and incipient militarism of a Howard Hawks, of the slick evasions of a *Bridge on the River Kwai* or *The Professionals*. *The Wild Bunch* is set at a point in time when society is increasingly institutionalizing and rationalizing the function of the unsocialized group. In terms of the radical structure of the film, the criminal is being supplanted by a criminal society. What distinguishes Peckinpah's 'heroes' from those who pursue them and those they traffic with is an extraordinary personal expertise and a fragile code of brotherhood, the two elements of their identity as the 'Wild Bunch'. If the Gorch boys are appetites and instincts, they are not vultures like the bounty hunters. Above all they are *brothers*, sharing a natural relationship rather than living out of principle. The threat their greed and violence pose to the unity – and hence the identity – of the Bunch is appropriately expressed through the constant friction between them and the two key characters, Sykes and Angel. Embodying the past and the conscience of the Wild Bunch, the old Sykes is created by Peckinpah as a mocking ('my what a Bunch') liability, ever threatened by Tector, finally left to die in the mountains when wounded by the bounty hunters. Angel is similarly opposed to the Gorch boys by virtue of his impulse (as in the assistance he provides to his village) to *extend* the ideal by which the Bunch try to live. Outside law, society, politics – 'we're not *associated* with anyone' – the Wild Bunch have but two choices for survival: they can give way to complete brutalization by serving a corrupt society, or can embrace the vision and future that Angel's simple communism offers. The tragedy is that the Bunch do neither, making the right choice for the wrong reasons.

At the centre of the group are Pike and Dutch, both holding it together and in the trust and affection of their relationship embodying the spirit that allows both Angel and the Gorches to belong. Of course the Bunch are not moral men: Dutch's self-deception ('we don't *hang* nobody') should not obscure the evidence everywhere before our eyes. In particular Peckinpah emphasizes that the Bunch attack women, Bishop trampling a young girl in his escape

Angel, 'the innocent vision of *The Wild Bunch*', and Pike Bishop, 'a crippled man burdened by his past'.

from San Rafael, the Gorches callously using them, Dutch shielding himself with a woman in the final massacre. Angel apart, the Bunch have no honour, only a way of life that is shared. Central to meaningful survival is *discipline*. *The Wild Bunch*, like *Major Dundee*, develops through a structure of divisive moments of impending violence alternating with rituals of celebration (especially drinking and shared laughter) which reunite. And what dooms the group finally is not only the fact that they cannot change; neither can they sustain their ideal of a disciplined unity.

It is Pike Bishop who is in every respect the leader of the Wild Bunch; and Bishop, like other Peckinpah heroes, is a crippled man burdened by his past. 'When you side a man you stay with him . . . if you can't do that you're worse than some animal.' Bishop asserts a value and an idea of himself that he is forced at every turn to compromise. 'Why didn't you tell me he was your grandson?' That the slow-witted Crazy Lee, left behind to die in Starbuck, is of Sykes's blood ironically points the issue, Bishop betraying the very history of the group. The execution of the blinded Buck, the acceptance of Angel's fate, the abandonment of Sykes himself: these acts develop the pattern of counterpoint between ideal and reality. The irony of the entrance of the Bunch, and their masquerade as a unit of soldiers, grows in this context. For Bishop this pattern has a special meaning, the vehemence of his commitment to the code informed by failure in the past ('being sure is my business'), Deke Thornton left behind when a trap had been sprung on them in a bordello. Peckinpah's characters are always caught in the grip of their own instincts, the demands of man's law, the dictates of God's. The tragedy springs from the fact that we cannot serve them all. Hence the strange bondage of Thornton, Harrigan's 'Judas goat', bound by his word to see his closest friend dead. At the end Thornton marches straight to Bishop's body and silently takes his gun: both recording the end of an era and an act of love, the moment also marks Thornton's freedom.

'Angel dreams of love while Mapache eats the mango.' Like Elsa of *Ride the High Country*, Angel is the spiritual centre, the innocent vision, the imperilled values, of the world of *The Wild Bunch*. Angel's complete loyalty to himself and 'family ties', his killing of Teresa in the lion's den, his commitment to 'my people, my village, Mexico', these cannot but describe a world of action for Bishop that his own life touched and departed from. The idea is sustained by another aspect of Pike's past, his love for the woman he hoped to marry blasted by her husband out of malice rather than jealousy, Bishop himself still limping from that wound of long ago. This delicate network of meaning is extended by the quiet moment Pike shares with a prostitute before the final battle, the scene carrying a bitter sense of what could have been, and suggesting a capacity for love untapped. The scene also recalls Pike's escape from the bordello, the wounded Thornton left behind. In this light Bishop's decision to return for Angel is classic Peckinpah action, the movement of a man into his past, a reassertion of identity, an honouring of the most important of contracts, that with one's self, God's law.

The great force of *The Wild Bunch*, as with *Major Dundee*, flows from its attack on the audience through Peckinpah's brilliant orchestration of the romantic drive of the genre, the viewer both exalted and violated. With the march of Pike and Dutch, Lyle and Tector, back into Agua Verde to confront Mapache, the transcendentalism of *Ride the High Country* is left far behind. As the group step out past the drunken soldiers and the huddled family groups, as our whole world hangs in suspense after the death of Mapache, as the bloody slaughter begins and grows and grows, as Lyle howls out his joyful song of blood-lust, as the Gorches die, their bodies endlessly dancing in the air, as Pike and Dutch finally expire after having 'done it right this time', as the bounty hunters sweep in to observe in hushed tones that history has been done ('T.C. – there he is . . . there's *Pike*'), as the film ends and Peckinpah, still unable to leave them, reprises the Wild Bunch to stop the picture with their ride out under the sunny trees of Angel's village, during and after all of this we cannot but experience the most painful confusion of feelings. *The Wild Bunch* succeeds in arousing in us precisely the world that it explores: an atavistic pleasure, a militant glee, a tragic sense of waste and failure. *The Wild Bunch* is a work of great audacity, a violent gauntlet at the feet of the liberal establishment of America. With this bleak and desperate film, the dialogue is now finished, the vision dead.

If the group honours its bond, if the spirit embodied in Sykes and Thornton is free to find what had always been its proper home ('even the worst of us . . .'), in the revolution, it is the unrelenting nihilism and despair, the absurd gratuitousness ('Why *not*?') of the action of the Wild Bunch itself that we are left with. For the Bunch it is too late, and history – their own way of life compromised rather than extended in a changing world – has gone too far. Finally the group act not for Angel's values – the 'dream of love' – but for the dead Angel, their own inadequate code, the *past*. More simply, they do what they do because there is nowhere to go. The Wild Bunch represent a way of life, a style of action, a *technology*, with no vision, no values, no goals. The quiet battle-cry of the group is, ironically, 'Let's *go*': but we can only ask *where*? In this context, although this great work is not the structured parable that *Major Dundee* is, we must see in it another chapter in Peckinpah's deeply troubled commentary on his country. *The Wild Bunch* is America.

Sam Peckinpah's West

As Dave Blassingame knees an opponent in *The Westerner*, the Englishman gasping that the blow is against the rules, the hero bellows: 'IT'S NOT A GAME!' Samuel Fuller's description of the cinema in Godard's *Pierrot le Fou* – 'a battlefield' – could well stand for Peckinpah's view of life. Certainly, his West is the dialectical frontier that runs between brutalizing instinct and self-defining discipline and action. The quest for personal identity is here equated with a movement towards inner peace and salvation. The Garden and Desert are not images of temporal life, but states of spiritual being, a choice for all men. To see Peckinpah simply as a moralist is to simplify and blur his work. There is an undeniable moral commitment in his insistence on self-knowledge as a prerequisite for meaningful action (*The Wild Bunch* is nothing if not moral); but in the end his unremitting vision of tortured souls caught up in an odyssey of self-exploration is a spiritual one.

In this, as in the Old Testament quality of many of his characters and images, we may sense a strong current of Puritanism, an inward concern with the struggle for deliverance from all evil. And certainly, although he is the most contemporary of directors in his use of the genre, Peckinpah is deeply rooted in and, like his heroes, oppressed by the American past. Here, as in so much else, he recalls John Ford; though where the older figure began by printing the legend and ended by bitterly trying to print the facts, Peckinpah's vision incorporates at once myth and reality, romance and tragedy. At times Peckinpah can create a cinema of great charm, intimacy and pastoral lyricism. These qualities, so prominent in *Ride the High Country*, are again uppermost in *The Ballad of Cable Hogue*, a poignant love-story with which Peckinpah is entering a second phase of his career after the obsessive efforts of the years given over to *Major Dundee* and *The Wild Bunch*. As these two works make clear, his other great strength is an epic and tragic sweep rooted in the commitment to test American tradition against present realities. If Peckinpah is progressively emerging artistically as John Ford's bastard son, it is because as an artist he is caught between the dream and the mango, the vision and the violence. The radical quality of his work – so evident in the distance between Ford's cavalry and his, between the activity on the horizon of Ford's heroes and Peckinpah's Wild Bunch, between the humour of Ford's stock company and that of the younger man's emerging repertory (Warren Oates, L. Q. Jones, Strother Martin, Ben Johnson) – arises naturally and inevitably from a deep personal romanticism which he fights every step of the way. And it is this tension which gives his cinema its distinctive allegorical quality, the present igniting the past, the promise and pain of America brought alive on the screen.

Peckinpah's talent is great. I have already referred to his skill as a writer; but of course this is more than a sensitivity to language. In particular there is his notable structural intelligence: he finds and inflects the forms that the breadth of his vision demands. One great danger will always be that his thematic drive, his commitment to the inner core of the work, may tend to out-strip narrative considerations. Another, of course, is his greatest strength, the uncompromising integrity and maverick reputation that resulted in the idleness following *Major Dundee*. That he is working again is no evidence of mellowing. Even with *The Wild Bunch* he is not completely happy ('96 per cent'); in particular he mourns the loss (in the domestic version) of the important flash-back that establishes the meaning of Bishop's bad leg, as well as the excision of a brief image evoking the Mexican way of life, a friendly butcher in his bloody open-market stall. If anything, Hollywood in its great need for talent to stay abreast of new audiences has changed more than Peckinpah. If he compromises now, it is on his own ground rather than the industry's.

Peckinpah's rare quality is the formal invention he brings to the service of his ambitious thematic range. In this, as Alan Lovell has pointed out, he suggests the stature and scope of a Jean Renoir. That he makes good his effects follows from the great care he exercises over every aspect of the production from casting to cutting. This concern results in significant detail in the finished work – the raven on Henry's shoulder, the portrait of Lincoln in Dundee's office, the hand-bill on Lyle Gorch ('Rapist; murderer') – which gives it his characteristic richness. His response to landscape typically reveals a careful geographical sense, while simultaneously creating an unearthly terrain, a Dante-like world over which his tortured characters move; here especially his distinctive, virtually baroque colour-sense comes into play. Still forming, Peckinpah's style seems marked by a heightened, often florid imagery held in check by the editing. Although imagery is often continuous with its own depth and play of light – as in the village sequences in *The Wild Bunch*, so reminiscent of Ford – increasingly Peckinpah's appears a cinema of montage, the flow of cutting both honouring and distending time, bridging all the elements of his action.

With a historical sense that demands the creation of character and community in the round, a social awareness that forces a contemporary relevance, and a metaphysical perspective that orders all, Peckinpah is by far the most compelling film-maker to have emerged from Hollywood in the past ten years. Working within the 'American genre, *par excellence*' in André Bazin's phrase, he has used the language of the western to explore and dramatize themes and conflicts obsessing the American sensibility. If this has been a traditional function of the western, Samuel David Peckinpah can be said to be bringing the genre up to date.

Filmography: Sam Peckinpah

Sam Peckinpah was born in 1926 in California. He gained a Master's degree in Drama at the University of Southern California, then worked in the theatre as director and actor. He went to KLAC-TV as a stage-hand. After two years he got a job as dialogue director with Don Siegel, and worked on thirteen pictures at Allied Artists in one year.

Television Work

Gunsmoke, 20th Century-Fox Hour, The Westerner, The Rifleman, Broken Arrow, Dick Powell Show (Pericles on 34th Street and *The Losers), Klondike, ABC-TV 'Stage 67' (Noon Wine).*

Scripting

Rewrite of *Invasion of the Body Snatchers* (Don Siegel, 1956). Scripted *The Glory Guys* (1966, director Arnold Laven) and *Villa Rides!* with Robert Towne from the novel by W. D. Lansford (1968, director Buzz Kulik).

Films directed by Peckinpah
The Deadly Companions (1961)

Production Company	Pathé-America-Carousel
Producer	Charles B. FitzSimons
Director	Sam Peckinpah
Script	A. S. Fleischman, based on his own novel
Director of Photography	William H. Clothier (filmed in Panavision)
Colour Process	Pathé Color
Editor	Stanley E. Rabjon
Music	Marlin Skiles
Sound	Robert J. Callen

Maureen O'Hara (*Kit Tilden*), Brian Keith (*Yellowleg*), Steve Cochran (*Billy*), Chill Wills (*Turk*), Strother Martin (*Parson*), Will Wright (*Doctor*), Jim O'Hara (*Cal*), Peter O'Crotty (*Mayor*), Billy Vaughan (*Mead*), Robert Sheldon (*Gambler*), John Hamilton (*Gambler*), Hank Gobble (*Bartender*), Buck Sharpe (*Indian*).

Running time: 79 mins. Original running time: 90 mins.
Distributor: Warner-Pathé.
First shown in Britain in 1962.

Ride the High Country (1961)

Production Company	M.G.M.
Producer	Richard E. Lyons
Director	Sam Peckinpah
Assistant Director	Hal Polaire
Script	N. B. Stone, Jnr
Director of Photography	Lucien Ballard (filmed in CinemaScope)
Colour Process	Metrocolor
Art Directors	George W. Davis, Leroy Coleman
Set Decoration	Henry Grace, Otto Siegel
Music	George Bassman
Sound	Franklin Milton

Randolph Scott (*Gil Westrum*), Joel McCrea (*Steve Judd*), Ronald Starr (*Heck Longtree*), Mariette Hartley (*Elsa Knudsen*), James Drury (*Billy Hammond*), R. G. Armstrong (*Joshua Knudsen*), Edgar Buchanan (*Judge Tolliver*), Jenie Jackson (*Kate*), John Anderson (*Elder Hammond*), L. Q. Jones (*Sylvus Hammond*), Warren Oates (*Henry Hammond*), John Davis Chandler (*Jimmy Hammond*), Carmen Philips (*Saloon Girl*).

Running time: 93 mins.
Distributor: M.G.M.
British title: GUNS IN THE AFTERNOON
First shown in Britain in 1962.

Major Dundee (1964)

Production Company	Jerry Bresler Productions
Producer	Jerry Bresler
Assistant to Producer	Rick Rosenberg
Production Manager	Francisco Day
Director	Sam Peckinpah
Assistant Directors	Floyd Joyer, John Veitch
Second Unit Director	Cliff Lyons
Script	Harry Julian Fink, Oscar Saul, Sam Peckinpah, from a story by Harry Julian Fink
Director of Photography	Sam Leavitt (filmed in Panavision)
Colour Process	Eastman Colour by Pathé. Print by Technicolor

Editors	William Lyon, Don Starling, Howard Kunin
Art Director	Al Ybarra
Special Effects	August Lohman
Music	Daniele Amfitheatrof
Title Song	Daniele Amfitheatrof, Ned Washington
Sung by	Mitch Miller's Sing Along Gang
Costumes	Tom Dawson
Sound	Charles J. Rice, James Z. Flaster

Charlton Heston (*Major Amos Dundee*), Richard Harris (*Captain Benjamin Tyreen*), Jim Hutton (*Lt Graham*), James Coburn (*Samuel Potts*), Michael Anderson, Jnr (*Tim Ryan*), Senta Berger (*Teresa Santiago*), Mario Adorf (*Sgt Gomez*), Brock Peters (*Aesop*), Warren Oates (*O. W. Hadley*), Ben Johnson (*Sgt Chillum*), R. G. Armstrong (*Rev. Dahlstrom*), L. Q. Jones (*Arthur Hadley*), Slim Pickens (*Wiley*), Karl Swenson (*Captain Waller*), Michael Pate (*Sierra Charriba*), John Davis Chandler (*Jimmy Lee Benteen*), Dub Taylor (*Priam*), José Carlos Ruiz (*Riago*), Aurora Clavell (*Melinche*), Begonia Palacios (*Linda*), Enrique Lucero (*Doctor Aguilar*), Francisco Reyguera (*Old Apache*).

Running time: 120 mins. Original running time: 134 mins.
Distributor: BLC/Columbia.
First shown in Britain in 1965.

The Wild Bunch (1969)

Production Company	Warner Brothers-Seven Arts
Producer	Phil Feldman
Director	Sam Peckinpah
Screenplay	Walon Green and Sam Peckinpah, from a story by Walon Green and Roy N. Sickner
Director of Photography	Lucien Ballard
Colour Process	Technicolor
Editor	Louis Lombardo
Art Director	Edward Garrere
Music	Jerry Fielding

William Holden (*Pike*), Ernest Borgnine (*Dutch*), Robert Ryan (*Thornton*), Edmond O'Brien (*Sykes*), Warren Oates (*Lyle Gorch*), Jaime Sanchez (*Angel*), Ben Johnson (*Tector Gorch*), Emilio Fernandez (*Mapache*), Strother Martin (*Coffer*), L. Q. Jones (*T.C.*), Albert Dekker (*Harrigan*).

Running time: 145 mins.
Distributor: Warner-Pathé.
First shown in Britain in 1969.

5: Postscript

Reacting away from a film journalism promiscuous with its praise and damnation, *auteur* critics by and large have taken up a descriptive and interpretative method aimed at evoking representative qualities. However, in the end criticism must confront the idea of value. The complexity of the problems of evaluation are obvious if we compare Mann and Boetticher. Holding broad thematic terrain in common, the two proceed in significantly different ways. Where Mann consistently increases the size of his canvas, Boetticher, the good genre painter, restricts and refines. Can we measure ambition or vision by the sweep of the work? The smaller the form, the greater control possible: hence the intense aesthetic pleasure Boetticher affords. The greater the form, the more likelihood of exciting the passions; yet size inevitably militates against perfection. Needless to say, the form itself is no measure either of seriousness or quality: certainly it is not clear to me that Mann is the more important artist. If anything, these two disparate figures seem (thus far) on a par at the middle range of achievement if we consider the extent to which the artistic vision has been fully explored. Judgement of Peckinpah must wait, as it should. Yet by these standards, his achievement could be great. The contradictions here are profoundly ironic: in unmasking and confronting them Peckinpah has already produced work of deep imaginative power.

The problems posed by genre are no less difficult, as I have

'*The Wild Bunch* is America'

found in writing this book. Yet the rewards seem to me considerable. As a critic whose roots are in education, I cannot believe, for
instance, that the tradition of the western must not occupy a central
place in film and cultural studies. In an increasingly utilitarian age,
one of film technology and 'participational media', the word 'art'
can seem to have a narrow and effete ring to it. Yet to study the
art of the western in any depth, we must embrace both mass
culture and the individual film-maker, the industry and the star,
film history, American history, and film language. Moreover, for
anyone interested in understanding America and its ideas of itself,
at corporate and deeply personal levels, the form is indispensable.

Tragedy, comedy, fable, allegory . . . it would be invidious to
paraphrase Polonius and claim the western was best for all modes.
Yet to continue to speak in unscholarly fashion of 'the western', or
to refuse to speak of it at all, is equally indefensible. Because they
have not been Ford, both Mann and Boetticher have gathered dust

in some camps. In others they have been torn from their context to be claimed as social and moral directors, if still to continue unexamined. In such a context it has seemed to me that a greater awareness of genre can assist in building the bridges, and furthering the dialogue, that our criticism so urgently needs.

Acknowledgements

I am grateful to Peter Wollen and Alan Lovell, former colleagues in the Education Department of the British Film Institute, for their support and ideas; in particular I must acknowledge their influence over the introduction. Anita Kitses and Paddy Whannel both read various sections of the manuscript and made valuable suggestions. Research materials were generously made available by Budd Boetticher, Gillian Hartnoll, Sam Peckinpah, James R. Silke, Brian Scobie and Chris Wicking. I am indebted to Susan Bennett for translations and preparing the filmographies, and to Dinah Connard and Jennifer Norman for assistance with research and typing sections of the manuscript.

This book is for my father and mother, John and Anastasia Kitses.

J.K.